Tennessee Political Humor

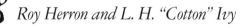

Roy Herron and L. H. "Cotton" Ivy

Tennessee Political Humor

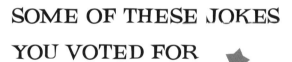

SOME OF THESE JOKES

YOU VOTED FOR

The University of Tennessee Press / *Knoxville*

The paper used in this book meets the minimum requirements of ANSI/NISO
Z39.48-1992 (R 1997) (Permanence of Paper). The binding materials have been
chosen for strength and durability.

Library of Congress Cataloging-in-Publication Data

Herron, Roy.
    Tennessee political humor : some of these jokes you voted for / Roy
Herron and L. H. "Cotton" Ivy.– 1st ed.
        p.   cm.
Includes bibliographical references (p.   ) and index.
    ISBN 1-57233-102-X (cl.: alk. paper)
    ISBN 1-57233-103-8 (pbk.: alk.paper)
1. Tennessee—Politics and government—1951—Humor.
2. Tennessee—Politics and government—1951—Anecdotes.
3. Politicians—Tennessee—Humor. 4. Politicians—Tennessee—Anecdotes.
I. Ivy, L. H. II. Title.
F440 .H47 2000
320.9768'02'07–dc21

                                                            00-009340

This book is dedicated to our boys and our brides. Our seven sons (that's four and three, not fourteen) and two wives (just one each) have blessed us more than we can say. They know up close and best just how humorous two Tennessee public servants can be.

Contents

Acknowledgments

The authors give special thanks to Pat Ivy and Nancy Miller-Herron who have lived with us despite our involvement in public life. We thank our sons, Jan, Bob, Vic, and Tim Ivy, and John, Rick, and Benjamin Miller Herron. They have inspired us daily and patiently endured our being away on state business or campaign trails.

We gratefully acknowledge our constituents, who have tolerated us kindly, helped us mightily, and been far better to us than we deserve.

We thank colleagues in and around all three branches of local, state, and federal governments who have shared special experiences, told funny stories, and tolerated our stories whether funny or not. Some are acknowledged in the notes and stories. Others who sought anonymity know who you are, but we hope no one else will.

We especially thank Vice President Al Gore and Governor Ned McWherter for their examples as public servants, their kindnesses, and their good humor. We greatly appreciate our friends Clark Jones and Johnny Hayes for demonstrating that politics at its best is helping others and having fun doing so. We also are much indebted to champion tale-tellers and political historians Joe Hill and Charlie Todd, both of whom helped us start on this book.

The University of Tennessee Press in general and Jennifer Siler, director, and Scot Danforth, editor, in particular have been exceptionally helpful and very patient. We have long loved our alma mater, but now we especially appreciate its fine press.

Larry Daughtrey of Nashville's *Tennessean* and Sam Venable of Knoxville's *News-Sentinel* have provided many insightful comments that much improved this work. We also appreciate Mark Byrnes's suggestions.

Ann Toplovich, executive director of the Tennessee Historical Society, has shared counsel and directed us toward needed resources.

Randy Eller of Eller's Bookstore in Nashville shared historical and research insights.

M. Lee Smith, Brad Forrester, and Ed Cromer of the *Tennessee Journal* have kindly allowed the use of their reporting and witticisms. Bruce Dobie of the *Nashville Scene* has done the same. Peachtree Publishers, Ltd., graciously allowed use of anecdotes from *They Love a Man in the Country* by Billy Bowles and Remer Tyson. Archivists Ken Fieth of Nashville's Metro Archives and Susan L. Gordon of the State Library and Archives provided invaluable assistance in locating photographs.

We are indebted to the Capitol Hill reporters, especially Duren Cheek, Rebecca Ferrar, Tom Humphrey, Rick Locker, Karin Miller, Tom Sharp, Don Spain, Paula Wade, and Phil West. And the incomparable icon, Drue Smith. These folks don't take elected officials too seriously and remind us we should not either.

Helpful readers include Josephine Binkley, Bob Cooper, Dennis and Jan Miller Dugan, Emmett Edwards, Ben Herron, Betsye Herron Hickman, Joe Hill, Brent Holmes, Mike Kopp, Tom Lee, Lucian Pera, and Byron Trauger. Bill Haltom is the best humorist writing in Tennessee, and his influence can be found throughout these pages.

A special thanks to our good friend Professor Walter Haden of UT Martin for his corrections and improvements. Neda Rachels and her son Ben prepared the index. John Lankford verified the notes and sources.

Friends who helped hammer (or at least key) the manuscript into shape include Joanne Pierce, Mary Gardner Simpson, Dixie Dorton, Tammy Frazier, and Sonya Pedigo.

Finally, we thank all those whom we have been privileged to listen to, learn from, laugh with, and love.

Introduction

Why a book of Tennessee political humor?

There are several reasons, including, among others, people in politics believe in laughter. The book of Proverbs instructs, "Laughter doeth good like a medicine."[1] As the most famous native of Grinder's Switch, Tennessee, the Grand Ole Opry star Minnie Pearl, used to say, "Laughter is God's hand on the shoulder of a troubled world." As a couple of Tennesseans who have served in government wrestling with some of the problems of that troubled world Minnie Pearl mentioned, we know what a blessing laughter can be. And we wanted you to laugh, too. So, that's why a book of *humor.*

Secondly, we gathered and created *political* humor because it is some of the funniest. Folks have been laughing heartily with and at Tennessee politicians at least since the 1820s and 1830s, when David Crockett ran for militia colonel, the Tennessee House of Representatives, and the United States Congress. Crockett was a tall tale teller who set the standard not only in Tennessee but also far beyond.

Third, we gathered *Tennessee* political humor because we are blessed to be Tennesseans. We enjoy our state's people, appreciate our storied history, and are thankful for the Tennessee tale tellers who have gone before us. After all, Congressman David Crockett started a national tradition that has continued through two centuries and now has entered a third.

But as our state enters the twenty-first century, much of that tradition and many of those tales from the twentieth century were in danger of being lost forever. Many of the humorous happenings were not written or recorded and need to be preserved. This book begins, we hope, to save those stories not only for our generation but also for those to come.

Also, many of the best tales that had been recorded were scattered in various biographies and old newspapers, inaccessible to most and handy to none. We did not want to gather the oral tradition and exclude wonderful written stories that were not readily available to all. So, we included the best of those tales, too.

Fourth, but perhaps most importantly, political humor often puts politicians in their place. We all take particular pleasure in laughing at folks foolish enough to try to be elected. As we ran for office, we eventually realized we were wisest, or least dumb, when we acknowledged our own foolishness. Wise are officials and candidates who tell the jokes and truth on themselves—before others do.

The humorist Grady Nutt used to say, "If you don't think God is a humorist, you need to look in the mirror every now and then." We say to others in politics and ourselves, if after looking in the mirror you still cannot laugh, then at least you will know what everyone else is laughing at. These stories hold the mirror up for officials to see what the rest of the electorate finds humorous.

These are the best pearls of humor we have found in Tennessee politics and government. Few of these stories are perfect, but then again, neither are your government and those of us you elected.

One historical imperfection is that a few times we have had to change the names. As the old television program *Dragnet* used to warn, "The names have been changed to protect the innocent." When we started telling public officials we were gathering tales for a book, we found we had to take the opposite approach. "The *innocent* don't need protecting," we told folks. "We're changing names to protect the *guilty*." In a few instances, we protected the reputations of the guilty and the feelings of their families and heirs. We also tried to protect ourselves, lest some family member sue us based on the mistaken belief that "Daddy *couldn't* have!" We have noted where names have been changed.

The vast majority of stories, however, use real names. Where important, we give historical context and basic biographical information. But, quite frankly, we have not wanted to interfere with your enjoyment or the stories themselves by inserting information that impedes the flow and may not be of interest. In the sources section at the back of the book, we indicate where we got each anecdote. We include endnotes for some direct quotations, and especially when multiple sources for particular stories are used. Other endnotes in-

clude background material and some amplifications. We also include
a bibliography, so you can easily match a shortened source note with
a fuller citation to find the whole work.

For more information about particular characters or contexts, we
recommend starting with *The Tennessee Encyclopedia of History and
Culture,* edited by Carroll Van West and created by the Tennessee
Historical Society.[2] Other useful works on Tennessee history include
Tennesseans and Their History[3] and *Tennessee: A Short History.*[4] For more
on Tennessee government, consider *Tennessee Government and Politics:
Democracy in the Volunteer State.*[5]

There are many books on political science and political issues,
public policy, and public administration. There are books on how to
win elections and books on how to govern. There are biographies of
public figures and historical works on public servants. There are even
books of photographs taken by and of public figures.

But few books reveal, much less revel in, what makes politics and
public service lively and fun. There simply are not many books of
political humor. This may be the first book of *Tennessee* political humor since Congressman David Crockett's autobiography, written almost two centuries ago.

You can say what you will about elected officials (and you probably already have), but Tennesseans often elect fine folks to office. The
public officials we have known usually have been as good as the citizens who elected them. (Some would say that's faint praise, but we
strongly disagree.) Granted, there are exceptions and some might
maintain we are two of them. Even so, most public servants work
harder and longer for less pay and more grief than they would if they
had chosen to remain outside public service.

Why do they do it? Most do it because neighbors have nurtured
and blessed them and they live in communities that care about them.
Most do it because they want to give something back to those who
have given so much to them.

How do they do it? Only by the grace of God and with a sense of
humor. Often with jokes, occasionally with pranks, frequently by
seeing the humor in humanity, not infrequently by revealing their
own funny flaws.

Our mothers used to tell us, "Sometimes you have to laugh to keep
from crying." It is the same with politicians and people in public

life. When the issues are hard, the hours long, the grind wearing, humor can be the salve that eases tensions and the grease that keeps the cogs of government moving.

Humor also helps public servants connect with those they serve. Caring officials want to bring down barriers and touch people. Often the quickest and most effective way to reach out is to confess a funny flaw, tell a tall tale, share a witty thought, or lay out a laugh line.

People running for office use humor for various purposes.

Some use humor and wit to ridicule and attack political adversaries. For example, Gov. Gordon Browning attacked challenger Frank Clement for proposing policies that were already being undertaken by Governor Browning's Administration, saying, "This candidate has come out for so many things already in effect, I would not be surprised if he came out for the Ten Commandments and the Sermon on the Mount before he gets through campaigning."[6]

On the other hand, Boss Crump of Memphis took out a newspaper advertisement claiming that Browning's heart had beaten over two billion times without a single sincere beat.

Other times, the humor is gentler, but still makes the point. One of our opponents told of going by a house with a sign saying "Democratic puppies for sale," but then a few days later the word "Democratic" had been marked through and replaced by the word "Republican." The opponent claimed the owner explained to him that they were the same puppies, but now their eyes were open.

Other times, those running for office and elected officials use humor not to attack but rather to embrace. Cotton's tall tales in the last chapter are examples of this use.

Sometimes people elevate politicians, particularly in higher offices, and put those politicians above themselves. The elected officials can come off those pedestals through self-deprecating humor. Such humor removes the distance, and dismisses any ideas that the politicians are aloof or distant. Various officials have told similar stories about campaigning and getting their comeuppance. One Tennessean told of introducing himself to a store owner and crew sitting around the stove in the country store and explaining he was running for office. Came the quick reply, "Yeah, we were laughing about that just this morning."

We acknowledge that most of this humor is by and about white males, since they have made up most of Tennessee's elected leadership. For example, all of Tennessee's governors and U.S. senators have been white males. Most legislators and other elected officials have been the same. We have contacted and sought to include women and racial minorities. Perhaps many realized inclusion in these tales is not necessarily a compliment.

Other issues arise when changing the spoken word into the written word. If the speakers had known their children and ours would read their remarks, their sometimes salty language would have been more suitable for family entertainment. So, we have ameliorated offensive language by substituting dashes.[7]

A larger question is this: How do you convert the spoken words to the written page? How do you put on a page the inflections, the lyrical voice changes, the dancing face muscles, the bouncing, arm-swinging, and general merriment of a humorist masquerading as a legislator?

How do you capture the gravelly voice of Frank Gorrell, a lieutenant governor turned lobbyist, fundraiser, and kingmaker? How do you capture the preaching power of a charismatic young governor like Frank Clement? How do you convey Gov. Ned McWherter's solemness and the hilarity of that bear of a man who can make a room roar in laughter with a raised eyebrow or the twinkle of an eye?

The truth is you cannot. Or at least, we cannot. And we do not know anyone else who can.

Ideally, this work would be a videotape, and the people you could see would be the ones we describe, and the voices you could hear would be the original tellers themselves. Unfortunately, many are gone now. So, we share their stories and hope you can re-create their voices in your mind.

Read these stories out loud. Better yet, tell them out loud. Let your voice dive and soar, your eyebrows rise, and your mouth twitch. Don't suppress the laughter, because if you do, it may go back in and come out at the hips.

Finally, some have said to us words to this effect:

Roy, as a senator you should not give a political opponent or a legislative colleague some of your best tales to use as ammunition against you or your position on an issue. Cotton, part of your value as a humorist is that you are the only one who knows your tales, so don't give away what you could sell.

We appreciate these concerns of friends who care about us. We know they speak both sincerely and truthfully. But we also believe humor ought not be hoarded. And we know that the Tennessee treasure that follows is not really ours. Others have created most of it, and we simply have been witnesses, students, and retellers.

So, here it is. All we ask is that after the stories make you smile, you share that smile—and the tales that gave it to you—with others.

Statewide Elections: Mischief from Mountain City to Memphis

The following are stories of campaigns and elections for governor and U.S. senator. Some would say statewide elections are different now. After reading these, you may say, "I sure hope so!" But if some of the old-time antics are better history than democracy, still there are plenty of laughs here.

TENNESSEE'S WAR OF THE ROSES

In 1886, brothers Alf and Bob Taylor ran against each other for governor. Since it involved family members, like the famous military campaign in medieval England, the race was called "The War of the Roses." The Taylor household had been divided since the boys were young. Their father, a Methodist minister, served in Congress as a Whig. But their mother was the sister of a Democratic Speaker of the Tennessee House of Representatives who became a Confederate senator from Tennessee. During the Civil War, their father was a strong supporter of the Union. Their mother's sympathies were with the South. Some would say the brothers were born into, brought up in, and destined for conflict.

In June 1886, the Republicans met in Nashville and on the first ballot nominated Alf Taylor for governor. Two months later, the Democrats also met in Nashville. After fifteen ballots, they chose Alf's brother, Bob, as their nominee.

The brothers decided to campaign together. The two often shared a room and even slept in the same bed. The first of forty-one debates

Robert Love Taylor (at right on stage) and brother Alfred "fiddlin' for votes." In 1886 Bob defeated Alf in a race for governor known as the "War of the Roses." From *Frank Leslie's Illustrated News,* October 2, 1886.

was held in September in Madisonville. Bob declared, "I have a very high regard for the Republican candidate—he is a perfect gentleman because he is my brother."

In Chattanooga, a joint committee of Republicans and Democrats prepared a fine welcome. Then the brothers were allowed some time before each was to speak from their hotel balcony. Both brothers wanted to make the best speeches possible, and Alf had even prepared a totally new manuscript for the special occasion. Then he left the hotel briefly to visit friends. While Alf was visiting, Bob began his speech. Alf soon heard a familiar phrase. He listened a moment, then exclaimed, "Great Scott! Listen! He is quoting the text of my speech, word for word. . . ."

In fact, Alf's brother was delivering a familiar and beautiful speech, including such carefully crafted lines as these:

> The illustrious dreamers and creators in the realm of music, the Mozarts, the Beethovens, the Handels and the Mendelssohns, have scaled the purple steeps of the heaven of sweet sounds, unbarred its opal gates and opened its holy of holies to the rapt ear of the world. In their wonderful creations of melody they have given a new interpretation and a sweeter tongue to nature and an audible voice to the music of the stars. Surely humanity can never forget God or our civilization sink to a lower plane while their works endure.

Alf rushed to their room, but it was too late. The manuscript was gone. Bob had it, and he did not return it until he had read Alf's entire speech to the crowd.[1]

MORE ROSE WARS

Generally, the Taylor brother candidates sought to entertain crowds with music and witty remarks, rather than confuse people with issues. Both played the fiddle. While Alf was a better fiddler, Bob usually had the sharper wit.

On one occasion, Bob said that while they were both born of the same mother and nursed at the same breast, Alf's milk soured on him and made him a Republican.

In his last campaign speech, Bob told the crowd, "I say to you now that after all these eventful struggles I still love my brother as of old, with an undying affection—but politically, my friends, I despise him."

Bob won by 13,000 votes.

Alf, however, did not quit. The next election he won a seat in Congress where he served three terms. In 1921, he finally won a race for governor—when he was seventy-two!

GOVERNOR BEN HOOPER

In 1910, Ben Hooper sought his Republican Party's nomination for governor. A gentleman named Sanders stated that the objection had been made to Hooper that he was "not well enough known." Hooper dryly responded that he had heard that some of the other candidates were "too well known."

Apparently Hooper made his point, as he won the nomination and then was elected governor.

Former Governor Ben Hooper, whose autobiography he entitled *The Unwanted Boy*, speaks as then Governor Prentice Cooper listens. Metropolitan Nashville Government Archives, *Nashville Banner* Collection.

KEFAUVER'S NAME PROBLEM

Congressman Estes Kefauver of Chattanooga ran for the U.S. Senate in 1948. His coonskin cap was attractive to West Tennesseans, who knew their ancestors' congressman had been Davy Crockett. Kefauver's name, however, was not nearly so familiar.

One day a group of young Democrats was riding a bus and campaigning with Congressman Kefauver. The Congressman had just spoken to a good crowd at a court square in West Tennessee when a woman whispered to a young Democrat: "We're having a little trouble with his name in these parts. We've never heard the name *Keep off her* before."

KEFAUVER AND CRUMP

Congressman Estes Kefauver took on Boss Crump and his candidate in the 1948 U.S. Senate race. Crump fired away, as usual, with mean, tough newspaper advertisements. There was no attempt at subtlety. Crump broke up the hot text with bold headings such as "How Red Is Red," "A Shameful Record," "Championed Communist Witnesses," and "Defending the 'Reds.'" Crump compared Kefauver's denials that he voted the Communist Party line to "[t]he pet coon that puts its foot in an open drawer in your room, but invariably turns its head while its foot is feeling around in the drawer. The coon hopes, through its cunning by turning its head, he will deceive any onlookers as to where his foot is and what it is into. If the coon could talk, he would say: 'You have me wrong—I have made a mistake, look at my turned head. I am sorry about my foot. I couldn't see what I was doing.'"[2]

The Crump ad has been described as "vicious as any in American political history." Kefauver's first reaction was to joke, "The only thing Red about me is my redheaded wife."[3] But, he soon answered the charges in a special radio broadcast. Kefauver said in that speech: "This attack is neither unusual nor unexpected. It isn't unusual because Mr. Crump designates automatically anyone who opposes his candidates as either a 'Red,' a 'Communist,' a 'tool of the C.I.O.,' a 'Thief,' or some other type of blackguard."

Kefauver commented on Crump's coon analogy:

This animal—the most American of all animals—has been defamed. You wouldn't find a coon in Russia. It is one of the cleanest of all animals; it is one of the most courageous. . . . A coon . . . can lick a dog four times its size; he is somewhat of a "giant-killer" among the animals. Yes, the coon is all American. Davy Crockett, Sam Houston, James Robertson and all of our great men of that era in Tennessee history wore the familiar ring-tailed, coonskin cap. Mr. Crump defames me—but worse than that he defames the coon, the all American animal. We coons can take care of ourselves. I may be a pet coon, but I "ain't" Mr. Crump's pet coon.[4]

Overnight, the coon referred to by Crump in his ad became the famous symbol of the Kefauver campaign in 1948. The Kefauver campaign even got a live coon and took it on the road. Kefauver would introduce the coon to the crowd by pointing out that "this is a pedigreed West Tennessee coon. Notice his big bushy tail. This coon has rings in his tail, but I want you to remember I have no ring in my nose."[5]

E. H. "Boss" Crump, the dominant and some said dominating leader of Memphis and statewide elections, raises his hand, making sure no one misses seeing the man behind the throne. Directly in front of Crump is Governor Prentice Cooper and to Cooper's right is U.S. Senator Kenneth McKellar. University of Memphis Libraries/Special Collections Department.

The live coon became a pest and a bother, not only because of the problems involved in hauling it around, but also it got upset at the noise and applause at campaign stops. A wildlife expert warned Kefauver's campaign manager the animal would die if kept confined. As a result, the coon was released to avoid a public relations setback to the campaign. Its replacement was the now-famous coonskin cap.

BOSS CRUMP AND GOVERNOR BROWNING

While Kefauver may have gotten the best of the notorious "Boss" Crump of Memphis with regard to raccoons, the boss uttered the masterpiece in campaign put-downs. E. H. Crump was a legendary leader with few scruples about elections, but he had considerable creativity in crucifying a candidate he opposed.

Crump helped elect Gordon Browning as governor in 1936, but the two soon fell out. In 1938, Crump opposed and helped defeat Browning. Ten years later, Browning ran for governor again. The race in 1948 was six years before Crump's death, when he was starting

Governor Gordon Browning sounds off at a Democratic National Convention. Metropolitan Nashville Government Archives, *Nashville Banner* Collection.

to lose his political grip, but not his will to fight. Browning won the election, but not until after he felt the scorpion sting of Crump's customary full-page ad in the Memphis *Press-Scimitar.*

Crump didn't just haul off and call Browning a crook. He did call him that, and more, but unlike some less-talented political hacks, Crump did it with style:

> I have said before, and I repeat it now,
> that in the art galleries of Paris there are 27 pictures of Judas Iscariot.
> None look alike but all resemble Gordon Browning;
> that neither his head, heart nor hand can be trusted;
> that he would milk his neighbor's cow through a crack in the fence;
> that of 206 bones in his body there isn't one that is genuine;
> that his heart has beaten over two billion times
> without a single sincere beat.

HONEST ELECTIONS

Browning repeatedly told audiences how Crump and his organization stalwart, Will Gerber, had been observed one night in a cemetery getting names of "voters" to help beat Browning. Gerber was on his knees reading names from the tombstones and Crump was recording the names in a notebook. Browning then told the tale this way: "He came to one he couldn't read because the moss had grown up all over it.

"'Just put down any name,' Gerber said. 'I know there's a name here but I just can't read it.'

"'No, Willie,' replied Crump, 'you've got to have the right name. This has got to be an honest election.'"

GOVERNOR DUNN'S PREELECTION FIGHT

Late in the 1970 governor's race, the Democratic candidate, John Jay Hooker, thought he had Winfield Dunn, the Republican, right where he wanted him. Reporters from Nashville's *Tennessean* had learned that Winfield Dunn had slugged a man in Mississippi and been arrested. Without telling the story, Hooker began to ask at campaign stops, "Have you told it all, Winfield? Have you told it all?"

Dunn's staff members tried their best to shield Dunn from reporters to keep the story from coming out, but finally reporter Jerry Thompson of the *Tennessean* asked the question. Dunn admitted that a few years earlier he had punched a man who had insulted his wife, Betty.

The story ran in newspapers and on electronic media all across the state. When it did, Dunn supporter Bill Jenkins, the former Speaker of the House who now is a congressman, called Dunn's campaign manager, Lamar Alexander. Alexander claims that even in Nashville he could feel Jenkins's excitement on the other end of the telephone way up in East Tennessee.

"That story's worth a hundred thousand votes up here," Jenkins exclaimed. "A man *ought* to defend his wife. Why didn't you boys bring that out sooner?"

ALEXANDER'S WALK ACROSS TENNESSEE

In 1978 Lamar Alexander decided to walk across Tennessee to boost his campaign for governor. It was an extraordinary campaign tactic. Alexander himself described it this way:

> First reactions to the walk were, at best skeptical. . . . The first truck driver whose hand I tried to shake rolled up his window. One of my Upper East Tennessee campaign managers refused to meet me at the county line because he was embarrassed to be seen with a character who would walk through the winter rain wearing a red and black shirt. . . .
>
> [M]y father was a little embarrassed by the whole adventure, and my mother was sure that I would be hit by a truck. She was right. In Newport, on only the ninth day of my walk, a white pickup flipped me over its hood. "Oh my God," said the driver as she leaped from the truck and saw who was lying in the middle of Main Street with campaign brochures scattered all over. "Why did it have to happen in Newport?"

BULLDOG ASHE VERSUS AL GORE

Political symbols and mascots have been important in political campaigns for many years. In the second half of the twentieth century in Tennessee, we saw such symbolic clothing as U.S. Senator Estes Kefauver's coonskin cap and Governor Lamar Alexander's red-and-black checked shirt. Both men were elected, and many gave considerable credit to their symbols. There have been, however, less memorable symbols that were not so successful.

In 1984, Victor Ashe, previously a state senator and now Knoxville's mayor, ran for the U.S. Senate. His principal opponent was Congressman Al Gore. Ashe chose a bulldog as his symbol. It was a logical selection, given that Ashe was a considerable underdog and also that he really was determined, persistent, and pugnacious in fighting for his beliefs.

During the campaign, the Tipton County Registrar told of watching television one evening with her husband. About 10 P.M., after her husband had dozed off, a Victor Ashe advertisement aired. At that point, her husband awoke. He watched the ad, including Ashe speaking and closing with the bulldog barking. Just before falling back asleep, her husband said, "I'd rather have the dog."

Then Tennessee State Senator Victor Ashe (right) shows then U.S. Congressman Albert Gore Jr. the bulldog that Ashe carried across Tennessee during their 1984 race for the U.S. Senate. Metropolitan Nashville Government Archives, *Nashville Banner* Collection.

CANDIDATE MCWHERTER'S QUICK STOP

A young lawyer in East Tennessee was fired up about former Governor Winfield Dunn's chances of beating then Speaker Ned McWherter in the 1986 gubernatorial election. In numerous speeches at Republican rallies, he really tore into McWherter. Speaker McWherter saw the press clippings and got reports about the young lawyer's attacks. While McWherter was touring the state, going into every one of the ninety-five counties, he came to the town where the young lawyer had an office. When McWherter spotted the lawyer's sign in front of the office, he yelled for his driver to stop.

The driver quickly braked, not knowing what was going on, but afraid of proceeding any farther. McWherter jumped out of the van and headed toward the office. His aides scrambled to catch up, none knowing what was going on.

McWherter burst into the office and, without introducing himself or even saying "good morning," demanded to know where the

After fourteen years as House Speaker, Ned McWherter jump-started his 1986 gubernatorial campaign by proclaiming, "Swear me in, give me a cup of coffee, two vanilla wafers, and I'll be ready to go to work." Boxes of vanilla wafers began arriving from supporters across Tennessee and the nation. In this photo, Governor McWherter appears with his trademark and makes then Senator Al Gore roar. Metropolitan Nashville Government Archives, *Nashville Banner* Collection.

young attorney was. The startled secretary stuttered that he was on the phone. McWherter did not slow a step but just kept on going. He flung open the door to the lawyer's office, and without pausing McWherter told the young lawyer: "I'm Ned McWherter and you need to quit lying about me. And you need to quit right now!"

McWherter turned on his heel and went right back, past the same startled secretary, out of the office across the sidewalk and back into the van. As his aides again scurried to catch up, McWherter demanded: "Let's go!"

If the young lawyer's attacks continued, they must have been muted, since they were not read about or reported further.

SIGN PROBLEMS

In the 1986 gubernatorial campaign, Charlie Todd was working for then Speaker Ned McWherter. Todd was having sign problems. During the day, he and friends would put McWherter signs alongside the highways in Todd's home area in Wayne County. At night, opponents with four-wheel drive vehicles would swerve off the roads and run over the signs.

Todd found a friend with welding skills. The welder took stout iron pipes and made frames for the McWherter signs. He painted the iron pipes black, so they would not be visible at night.

Todd reports that it took just one pickup running into the iron posts to stop the drive-by destruction.

SLEEPING TIGHT TONIGHT

During the 1986 gubernatorial campaign, Charlie Todd also worked as an advance man for Speaker Ned McWherter. McWherter, a multimillionaire, was famous for being tight with money (which was, some noted, how he got to be a multimillionaire). He had commanded his campaign team: "Be economical." Todd, who knew something about being economical and also about the importance of pleasing his boss, took McWherter's instruction very seriously.

As Todd traveled and planned McWherter's itinerary, he therefore looked for motels that were economical. And he found some.

One night Todd had McWherter stay at a seventeen-dollar-a-room place where they were the only guests. Steve Browder, the highway patrolman assigned to the Speaker, pointed out to Todd: "Well, at least these rooms have phones. They don't have dials on 'em, but they are phones."

To use the phones, they had to get the motel manager to connect them. But since the motel was otherwise deserted, the manager did not stay around, so they could not even call out, much less receive calls.

After another night in one of Todd's economical motels (a relatively expensive one at nineteen dollars a room), as McWherter climbed in the car, Todd asked, "How'd you sleep, Mr. Speaker?"

McWherter replied, "Once I got the ants off of me, I slept all right."

"The *ants* off of you?" the shocked Todd replied.

"Yeah," McWherter replied. "About three in the morning I got up, showered to get 'em off of me, then jumped back in bed and got back to sleep as quick as I could, 'cause I knew they would be coming again."

But the high point, or perhaps one should say low point, came at a motel called "The Birdview."[6] Todd had arranged well in advance for three rooms for McWherter, Browder, and himself. Todd had explained that they would be arriving late, but the manager had assured him, "The key'll be in the door."

A little nervous about the arrangements and wanting to make sure everything was lined up, Todd had called back a week before the trip. The manager had reassured him yet again, "Don't worry. The key'll be in the door."

But, when Todd, McWherter, and Trooper Browder arrived about one o'clock in the morning, there was no key in any door. In the motel "office" Todd and Browder found piles of clothes. On the counter were a bra and a gun clip. Browder, the highway patrolman, nervously put his hand on his own gun, as Todd called out for the manager.

The manager eventually came into the room, his overalls partially up and holding one overall strap in his hand. He growled, "We ain't got no rooms."

"Awww man," Todd replied. "You *got* to have some rooms. I made the reservations. And I've talked with you twice about our staying here. I've got the Speaker of the House of Representatives out in the car and you've *got* to have some rooms."

Reluctantly, the manager begrudgingly consented to help them find rooms. Out went the manager, Browder, and Todd, walking past McWherter, who sat in the car, smoking his pipe, watching the whole episode. Todd figured McWherter was trying to decide whether to fire him right then or wait until they got back to Nashville.

The manager led Todd and Browder from room to room, looking in the windows, saying things like "Nope, somebody's in that one." Finally, three times, he said, "Looks like there's one for you." Then the manager said, "Now, if I can just find the keys."

The manager went back to the office and finally found keys for the three rooms. Todd and Browder ushered the weary McWherter to his room, then staggered to their own rooms.

Soon Browder knocked on Todd's door and pointed out that both beds in his room had been used and that the room contained the odor of the used but unflushed toilet. Browder complained it was not fit for any human and few beasts. Todd let Browder into his somewhat less rough room.

The next morning, Todd nervously asked, "Mr. Speaker, you okay?"

McWherter replied, "Todd, you've done good. You've been economical."

But as they started driving away, McWherter said to the highway patrolman: "Browder, hold it."

The trooper stopped the car. McWherter looked at Todd and said: "You know, Charlie, lots of times I like a drink of water in the morning."

"Yessir, I do, too."

"But it helps to have a glass to get the water, doesn't it?"

"Uh, yessir."

"Well, I didn't have a glass in my room."

"Sorry, Mr. Speaker."

McWherter nodded, and the patrolman pulled the car back on the road. They drove a ways, then McWherter told the trooper to stop again. He turned and looked at Todd again: "Charlie, the first thing I like to do in the morning is I like to take a shower."

"Me too, Mr. Speaker."

"But it helps if I have a bath rag. Or a towel. Or both. I didn't have either this morning, Charlie. So, I showered and then I had to use the sheet off the bed to dry off."

"Oh, sorry, sir."

McWherter shook his head and finally said, "Charlie, don't tell the rest of the staff, but you're just going to have to upgrade."

McWherter nodded and the trooper took off again. Todd was feeling pretty bad, and McWherter could tell it. Pretty soon he had the trooper stop again.

"Charlie, one other thing."

"Yessir, Mr. Speaker," Charlie replied, wondering what else could have gone wrong and thinking he was about to be fired.

"That place was called 'The Birdview,' wasn't it?"

"Yessir, I'm afraid it was."

McWherter finally smiled.

"Well, where the ———— were the birds?"

THEY WARNED ME

On the campaign trail in 1992, Senator Jim Sasser referred back to the presidential campaign of 1988. That earlier race had pitted Republican George Bush against Democrat Michael Dukakis. Bush won overwhelmingly. Four years later, however, Sasser would quip: "In 1988, a Republican friend told me if I voted for a Democrat for president, then there would be increased unemployment, a sour economy, tough times. I still voted for Dukakis, but my Republican friend sure was right!"[7]

THE CARD-PLAYING DOG

In 1996, Houston Gordon ran as a decided underdog against United States Senator Fred Thompson. During the race, Gordon repeatedly told this story:

A fellow from New York came down to the little community of Henning in rural West Tennessee. He stopped in the pool hall and bought a beer. As he looked around the pool hall, he saw a dog playing cards. He shook his head and made sure his eyes were not playing tricks on him. Then he went over to the man playing cards with the dog and asked: "Am I seeing this right? Is that dog playing cards?"

The man replied, "Yep."

The New Yorker was amazed. He went on and on. The West Tennessean finally had heard enough and told the New Yorker: "The dog's not really very good."

"What do you mean?" the astonished New Yorker asked.

"Well," the Southerner drawled, "when the dog gets a strong hand, he usually gives it away by wagging his tail."

Local Elections:
The Heart—and Funny Bone—
of Democracy

Former U.S. Congressman Tip O'Neill is often given the credit for the phrase "All politics is local." And much of the best election humor is local, too. Consider the following stories from Tennessee's local politicians and local elections.

THE SPOILS OF VICTORY

In the 1930s and 1940s, West Tennessee was solidly Democratic. Still, even then there was a Republican who was diligent and faithful. Even while Franklin Delano Roosevelt and Harry Truman held the White House for twenty years, this Republican labored hard, though in vain.

But with Eisenhower's victory in 1952, finally, the Republicans had won the presidency.

After the election it was time to reward this soldier who had labored so hard and so faithfully in such tough times. So the phone call was made to him down in Fayette County. The Republican Party operative who called thanked him for his diligent work and asked if there was anything that the party could do for him.

The old gentleman replied, "Yes, yes, there is."

"Well, tell me what you'd like. Whatever we can do for you, we surely want to do."

"Well, I really want to be the ambassador to the court of Saint James."

There was a stunned silence on the other end of the line. Finally, the party official replied: "You, you mean you want to be the ambassador to Great Britain?"

"That's right," replied the old man.

After more fumbling for words, the younger man told the would-be ambassador he would check on it and call him back.

Then the young man tried to figure out what to do. A colleague finally suggested that he call back and see if anything else might be acceptable to the faithful Republican soldier. When he called back and asked, the old man slowly replied: "Well, as a matter of fact, there is one other thing that might suit me as well."

The young man shuddered to imagine a request to become the ambassador to France or some other incredibly unreasonable appointment. But he mustered up the courage to ask "What else would that be?"

"Well, I hear they might be needing a new postmaster over at Moscow. Do you reckon I might be able to get that job?"

Very shortly thereafter, the Fayette County community of Moscow, population not many, had a new postmaster.

MY DAD BEING AN ELECTION OFFICIAL

My dear daddy used to tell what he swore was a true story. It happened when he served as an election official.

When a voter went to the polling place, voters walked up and said which primary they wanted to vote in. For example, someone would say, "I want to vote in the Democratic Primary." Then the local election officials used to judge that person. They would say, "Yeah, he is a Democrat" or "No, he isn't a Democrat, he's a Republican." Persons were not allowed to vote in a primary unless they were judged to be members of that party.

One day my father was working as an election judge, and a woman in her twenties came to vote for the first time. One of the election workers told her: "Ma'am, you're going to have to tell which party you affiliate with before you can vote."

The young woman seemed startled. She finally replied: "Well, I don't understand, but I'm going to tell you one thing. I can't and I ain't aiming to tell the party that I affiliate with."

The worker replied, "Well, why is that, ma'am?"

The woman hesitated, then said: "Well, mainly it's because he ain't divorced yet."

DOUBLE-CROSSED

In the late forties or early fifties, J. W. (Jaybird) Hill and Frank Ball ran against each other for chairman of the Henry County Road Board. Hill was from the town of Henry and Ball was from Paris. One of Jaybird's secret campaign workers was Mr. John Hurst "Hotie" Peebles of Henry. About ten days before the election, Hotie was in Paris where he ran into Jaybird's opponent, Mr. Ball. Not knowing that Hotie was a secret campaign worker for Jaybird, candidate Ball asked Hotie if he could help him get a few votes around Henry.

Hotie replied, "Well sure, Jaybird ain't gonna get all that many votes in Henry."

Encouraged, Ball asked, "Well, do you need any resources?"

Hotie replied that he thought he could get the job done "with a hundred dollars and a gallon of whiskey." Ball supplied the resources.

On election night hundreds gathered at the county newspaper, the *Paris Post-Intelligencer,* to watch the returns posted precinct by precinct on a big board. With every precinct accounted for except the box at Henry, Frank Ball was ahead by about 250 votes. Then came Henry. It was Hill with 408 and Ball with 26, reversing Ball's lead and giving the election to Jaybird Hill.

Frank Ball made a beeline to campaign worker Hotie Peebles of Henry and exclaimed: "Hotie, what the heck happened? You said you were gonna help me. Look on that board! Why, I didn't get hardly anything in Henry. Now here I am beat because I was depending on you. Will you please explain yourself?"

Hotie replied, "Looks to me like them ——— double-crossed me."

To this day some of the old time students of Henry County politics are still trying to decide exactly how Frank Ball's resources were used in that election.

BRAWN AND BRAINS

J. B. "Buck" Avery of Alamo was a huge man. In a race for district attorney general, Avery's chief opponent was Trenton attorney Limmie Lee Harrell, a man small enough to ride as a jockey in horse races at county fairs.

During the campaign, the candidates often appeared together. On one occasion, Avery spoke to the crowd first. To have some fun at the expense of his opponent, the large Avery commented that Harrell was "not big enough for the job."

"Why, if I wanted to," Avery boasted, "I could just eat him up in one bite."

When Harrell spoke, he wasted no time responding.

"Well, Mr. Avery might be able to gobble me up in one bite. But, if he did, he'd have a ———— lot more brains in his stomach than he's got in his big old head!"

The little man won the debate and the election.

THE SHERIFF'S REELECTION

There was a Tennessean who lived in a rural county. Though married, he seemed not much bound by the tie that binds, and he pursued women other than his wife. Despite his weakness, he was elected sheriff. But after he was elected, far from becoming a circumspect public official, he got worse. Indeed, he began to chase women with a passion seldom seen and an ardor rarely matched.

Then came time for his reelection. One day right before the election, he came out of the courthouse and saw a lifelong friend who was a rather proper member of the Baptist Church. The sheriff went up to his friend and said: "Charlie,[1] I need your vote in this election."

Charlie paused, then replied: "Sheriff, I must be honest—I will *not* vote for you."

The sheriff was shocked. "But Charlie, you are my lifelong friend! I have known you since we were children! You supported me in the last election. Why in the world will you not vote for me now?"

Again Charlie hesitated, but then he replied: "In a word, *morals.*"

The sheriff was stunned. "Morals? Morals? I haven't taken bribes. I've locked up the crooks. I've been tough on crime. I haven't stolen any money. What do you mean *morals?*"

His friend soberly and sternly replied: "You have tried to have your way with every woman in this town!"

Stung, the sheriff thought for a quick moment, then protested: "But, Charlie, this town ain't that big a town!"

ROSS BASS'S BEATING—AND WINNING

In 1954, Congressman Pat Sutton chose to leave his congressional seat to run against Kefauver for the U.S. Senate. A postmaster named Ross Bass ran for Sutton's seat in Congress.

Bass entered the campaign as a heavy underdog, but he made enough progress to scare critics. Two such critics were brothers who liked to take a drink or ten. After considerable consumption, one evening they attended a Bass rally. They began heckling Bass "zestfully and mercilessly" as Bass tried to speak to the crowd. Bass responded that his "momma would have taken [him] out and whipped [him] if he had acted like [them]." The brothers then jumped Bass. Before they could be pulled off Bass, the brothers injured his back, cut his wrist, and blacked his eye.

The next night, Bass drove to Nashville to go on television. Upon seeing Bass, anchorman Judd Collins offered him a steak for his eye and some makeup to hide his wounds. Bass, looking for public sympathy, firmly replied: "You touch that black eye and I'll kill you."

Bass later credited the attack for his 3,067-vote victory.

REPRESENTATIVE TOMMY BURNETT

Tremendously talented State Representative Tommy Burnett of Jamestown was sentenced to serve time in a federal prison in the 1980s for failing to file his federal income tax returns. He decided to run for reelection while still in prison.

While Representative Burnett was running (if that's the proper term for whatever one does in prison with one's name on the ballot in another state), a national newspaper reporter interviewed one of Burnett's Fentress County constituents.

The reporter asked whether the citizen was going to vote for Representative Burnett even though he was in prison. The reply was quick and certain: "Sure, I'm going to vote for him."

"Why, sir, are you going to vote for an imprisoned man?" the baffled reporter asked.

Came the fast explanation: "We've already sent one good man to the legislature—we don't want to ruin another."

Tennessee House Majority Leader S. Thomas Burnett (left) and long-time Finance Ways and Means Chair John Bragg study legislation on the floor of the Tennessee House of Representatives. Metropolitan Nashville Government Archives, *Nashville Banner* Collection.

ANOTHER BURNETT STORY

Shortly before that same election, prisoner and Representative Burnett called his oldest son, then still a high school student, who was serving as campaign manager. Representative Burnett happily exclaimed the good news that he might be released in time to come home before the election and he then would be able to campaign.

There was a long silence, then his son finally replied: "Dad, I've about got this thing won. Don't you get out and mess things up!"

REPUBLICAN PUPPIES FOR SALE

In 1986 we were both running for the legislature. A Republican opponent told the following story at a civic club.

I was out campaigning and came to a house that had a sign out front that said: "Democratic puppies for sale." So, I decided I would not waste my time seeking a vote there.

A few days later I came by the same house and the sign had been changed to read: "Republican puppies for sale."

Intrigued by the change, and more hopeful of finding a vote, this time I stopped. I knocked, and a man came to the door.

"Pardon me, sir," I said. "I noticed that you have changed your sign from 'Democratic puppies for sale' to 'Republican puppies for sale.' Do you have some new puppies?"

"Oh, no," the gentleman replied. "They're the same puppies. But now they've got their eyes open."

FIRST ONE SEEN UP CLOSE

In 1986, Bobby Carter first ran for the state senate. He went to Trenton to shake some hands and introduce himself to county officials in the courthouse.

Carter, a Republican, knew Trenton was "enemy territory" and very Democratic. But he bravely ventured forth. Of course, people in the courthouse were gracious and nice. Carter was starting to feel better about his chances. Then, as he walked out of the courthouse, he saw three elderly men sitting on a bench. Carter strolled over to give them his election card. After carefully scrutinizing Carter's card, one of the men looked up at Carter and asked, "Are you that thar *Republican* runnin' for office?"

Carter said he was.

The fellow gave Carter a thorough once over and finally said, "You're the first one of them I've ever seen up close!"

CAMPAIGN SIGN DESTRUCTION

When I (Cotton Ivy) first ran for the Tennessee House of Representatives, I enlisted the help of a devout Democrat in a rabidly Republican county. Charles G. Todd was one of Wayne County's most devoted Democrats, but he was a distinct, and some would say endangered, minority. But he bravely volunteered in my campaign. Among his responsibilities was erecting signs.

Charlie Todd soon learned that erecting the signs was not that difficult. But keeping them erect was. In fact, as soon as he put up my signs, they were torn down. It happened repeatedly. Finally, Todd thought he might have a solution.

Todd asked for help from a farmer friend with a large truck in which he hauled livestock. Todd also talked to another fellow with access to a large truck with a boom and a bucket, like those that hoist people up to work on light poles and phone lines. Soon the farmer was holding a ladder on top of the cab of his truck as his young son went up the ladder with baling wire to hang my signs in tall sycamore trees. The fellow with the bucket truck did the same thing. Shortly thereafter, all over the county my signs hung twenty-five and thirty feet in the air, shining down on people driving on the roads and especially as they stopped at intersections.

The signs drew much more attention in the trees than they ever had on the ground. And all the opposition could do was shoot at them. Which they did, but to little effect.

Most of those signs stayed in those trees for years, until they finally rotted and fell out.

A COUNTY EXECUTIVE'S POLITICAL ADVICE

Andy Smith served West Tennessee's Decatur County as its county executive. He once explained his campaign and political tactics this way. He said:

> You need to keep politics kind of quiet, the best you can.
> Don't ever write anything down when you can phone.
> Don't ever use that telephone if you can see someone face to face.
> When you see someone face to face, don't talk unless you have to.
>   Sometimes you can just smile.
> If a smile won't do it, sometimes just a wink will.
> And if you can get by with it, don't wink, just nod.

WHISKEY SPEECH

A classic in political humor is the "whiskey speech." The late Lieutenant Governor Frank Gorrell of Nashville often would give this speech to the great amusement of his many friends. It apparently originated with a Mississippi official named N. S. Sweat Jr. when he was asked his position on the hot issue of Prohibition. It has been enjoyed in various forms and at numerous forums in Tennessee for many years. Here is the classic statement of an elected official willing to take a stand and stand by it:

Friends:

I had not intended to discuss this controversial subject at this particular time. However, I want you to know that I do not shun controversy. On the contrary, I will take a stand on any issue at any time, regardless of how fraught with controversy it might be. You have asked me how I feel about whiskey. All right, here is how I feel about whiskey.

If when you say whiskey you mean the devil's brew, the poison scourge, the bloody monster, that defiles innocence, dethrones reason, destroys the home, creates misery and poverty, yea, literally takes the bread from the mouths of little children.

If you mean the evil drink that topples the Christian man and woman from the pinnacle of righteous, gracious living into the bottomless pit of degradation, and despair, and shame, and helplessness, and hopelessness, then certainly I am against it.

But:

—if when you say whiskey you mean the oil of conversation, the philosophic wine, the ale that is consumed when good fellows eat together, that puts a song in their hearts and laughter on their lips, and the warm glow of contentment in their eyes.

—if you mean Christmas cheer.

—if you mean the stimulating drink that puts the spring into the old gentleman's step on a frosty, crisp morning.

—if you mean the drink which enables a man to magnify his joy, and his happiness, and to forget, if only for a little while, life's great tragedies, and heartaches, and sorrows.

—if you mean that provider of dollars, which are used to provide tender care for our little crippled children, our blind, our deaf, our dumb, our pitiful aged and infirm; to build highways and hospitals and schools, then certainly I am for it.

This is my stand. I will not retreat from it. I will not compromise.[2]

REPRESENTATIVE GARRETT
ON PEOPLE NOT VOTING

When Representative Tim Garrett was elected in 1982, he studied the numbers of persons voting in his election. He carefully analyzed the statistics and determined that approximately 15,000 people could have registered to vote in his district. But only 8,000 had, in fact, registered. And only 4,000 had voted. Of those, 2,500 had voted for Tim and about 1,500 for his opponent. After he realized how few citizens actually elected him, he told his grandfather: "I could walk down the street and call every other person a ———— and still be in pretty good shape!"

PRAYERFUL ENDORSEMENTS

In 1998, Vice President Al Gore came to Tennessee and helped fourth district congressional candidate Jerry Cooper by attending a fundraiser. Meanwhile, in the adjacent third congressional district, former state senator Jim Lewis, also a Democratic nominee, was asked why the vice president had not also stopped to help him.

Lewis replied: "You'll just have to address that question to him. But let's assume that he's praying for me."

Legislative Branch:
The Unholy Trinity

"They just don't make 'em like they used to." We all have heard that expression many times. It may be most true about that group known as legislators. Perhaps in some ways that is good.

After all, when President Lyndon Johnson was a child and his father was a Texas legislator, lobbyists provided Texas legislators with "beefsteak, bourbon, and blondes." The railroads and other powerful interests in those days took care of legislators in many states, including perhaps even our own fair Tennessee. In those days of looser ways, however, President Johnson's father was thought of as a man of exceeding rectitude. It was not that he shunned places of ill repute or declined to participate in beefsteaks, bourbon, and blondes. It was that instead of letting the lobbyists and interests pay for his pleasures, Johnson paid for his own.[1]

Still, in other ways, the early and middle parts of the twentieth century really were "the good ole days." Or at least the humorous old days. In Tennessee, no period was more humorous than the one presided over by three legislators known affectionately as the "Unholy Trinity."

For many years the trio led Tennessee's legislature. All three were Middle Tennesseans, Cumberland University alumni, and country lawyers.

Jim Cummings was born in Cannon County in 1890, began law practice in his home town of Woodbury in 1922, and was first elected to the Tennessee House of Representatives in 1928. His fourteen terms in the House and four in the Senate totaled thirty-six years, longer than any previous state legislator in Tennessee history. A small man with a high voice, Cummings was always cheerful, but he was also shrewd, alert, and unmatched as a floor leader.[2]

I. D. Beasley of Carthage in Smith County teamed with Cummings as a floor leader. Born in 1895, Beasley first won a seat in the House of Representatives in 1920. He served twenty-six years in the General Assembly, eight terms in the Senate, and five in the House. Beasley and Cummings actually rotated between the Senate and House for many years. A bachelor, carrying 230 pounds on a five-foot, three-inch frame, Beasley has been described as perhaps the most colorful character to serve in the state legislature.[3] The "Mockingbird of Capitol Hill" could mimic anyone he heard speak, and Beasley became a legend for using that talent to play jokes on governors, visiting dignitaries, and other political leaders.

The third member of the trio, Walter "Pete" Haynes, was from Winchester in Franklin County. Haynes won his first race for the General Assembly in 1928 and served twenty-four years. He was Speaker three of his nine terms in the House and Speaker two of his three terms in the Senate. The skillful trial attorney served as the master parliamentarian and cloakroom intriguer for the Unholy Trinity.[4]

For almost forty years, Tennessee rural interests were upheld by these three dominant personalities in the General Assembly. They were as talented a trio as any recall and certainly equally colorful. Consider the following stories of the Unholy Trinity.

TAKING CARE OF HOME-FOLKS

Prior to the 1960s and the landmark United States Supreme Court decision of *Baker vs. Carr,* rural legislators from West and Middle Tennessee out-numbered East Tennesseans and urban legislators. These legislators controlled the legislature even though urban and east Tennesseans were a majority of the qualified voting population of the state. Leading these country legislators were the Unholy Trinity. As Mr. Jim Cummings noted, "We were three country lawyers connected by our interest in rural Tennessee."[5]

The sage of Woodbury voiced the rationale for protecting the countryside against the urban threat when he shared his simple philosophy: "We must not," he declared, "allow numerical concentrations of people to have too great a voice in government. It's not healthy . . . I believe in collecting the taxes where the money is—in cities—and spending it where it's needed—in the country."[6]

IN THE PENITENTIARY

Clarence Cummings and Barton Dement were well-known lawyer-legislators from Murfreesboro. Dement served in the legislature in the 1950s and 1960s. Cummings served in the Senate in the 1920s, but as the brother of long-time legislator Jim Cummings and friend of many legislators, long after his legislative service ended he still found his way to neighboring Nashville. His brother Jim happily recalled the following story about his brother and friend.

They went to Nashville and in the course of their day's work, they got to drinking, fooling around, overindulged. And they had some friend who was a guard out at the penitentiary.

As the night went on, "The guard realized that he needed to do something for my brother and Barton Dement. They were over-loaded. So he took them out there and bedded them down in his quarters at the state prison. They fell into a deep sleep, of course. And the next morning they woke up and looked out the window and saw they were inside the walls. Convicts were walking around.

"One of them said to the other, 'Whur in the ———— are we? WE'RE IN THE PENIT—THAT'S THE penitentiary. We're in the *penitentiary.*'

"Barton says, 'Clarence'—that's my brother's name—'Do you remember being put in here?'

"And Clarence said, '————, I don't even remember having a trial.'"[7]

REPRESENTATIVE I. D. BEASLEY
AND GOVERNOR COOPER

Representative I. D. Beasley, like his dear friend Representative Jim Cummings, was a short man, and nearly as wide as he was tall. If you were introduced to someone from Smith County, chances are the person, or his or her brother or sister or uncle or cousin, owed a job to Representative I. D. Beasley. The state employees in Smith County revered the short, obese, cigar-chewing rogue from Carthage.

One day, Governor Prentice Cooper was hurrying through Smith County when the state trooper chauffeuring his car slammed on the brakes at a roadblock. Standing in their way was an old man named Shaw, a state employee who, of course, owed his job to I. D. Beasley.

The trooper got out and tried to persuade old Shaw to let the governor through, explaining that they were on important state business and running late. While they argued, the governor got out of the car and rushed up to the barricade.

"You don't know who I am," he thundered. "I'm Prentice Cooper, the governor of Tennessee."

Shaw replied, "I don't give a ———— if you're I. D. Beasley, you're not going through here."

I. D. BEASLEY AND THE HARD-OF-HEARING D. A.

A stranger in Carthage once asked directions to the office of District Attorney General Baxter Key, one of Representative I. D. Beasley's close friends. Representative Beasley accommodated the stranger with directions, but falsely warned him that District Attorney Key was deaf and could hear only if you shouted directly into his ear at the top of your lungs.

General Key later recalled, "That was thirty years ago, and I can hear him yet."

I. D. BEASLEY'S VOTE AND PETE HAYNES

"I. D. Beasley was smart as a tack and was fearless, absolutely fearless, both physically and morally," recalled Joe Hickerson, Pete Haynes's law partner in Winchester.

When they both were in the legislature, Haynes approached Beasley to inquire how he planned to vote on a bill. Incensed, Beasley told Haynes it was none of his business and he didn't want to be told how to vote.

"Why, I.D., I'm not telling you how to vote," an amused Haynes replied. "I just want to know how you're going to vote. I've got you sold both ways and I've got to give one guy his money back."

THE UNHOLY TRINITY
AND THE UNHOLY PREACHER

The Unholy Trinity believed one of its missions was protecting the people of Tennessee from legislators who brought such foolish legislation as truck-weight limits and morality bills.

"There was a preacher in the Legislature, old man Ruffin from way down in West Tennessee, religious gentleman, who wanted all sorts of legislation to establish morals," Jim Cummings related. "He introduced every kind of ———— bill you can think of. One was to require that all hotels keep a night cop on every floor to keep improper and, uh, uh, uh, things from going on in the hotel. Had several bills along that line. Everybody hated him for it. Heck, nobody wanted that kind of ———— legislation."

Cummings said Ruffin lived in the Clark Hotel, a rooming house between the Capitol and the Hermitage Hotel where Cummings, I. D. Beasley, and Pete Haynes were staying.

"Old Ruffin would go to the penitentiary every Sunday and preach to the convicts, good old man," Cummings said. "Old Miss Clark ran the boarding house. She was a hard-as-nails and mean-as- ———— — old lady."

Governor Winfield Dunn unveils and Representative Jim Cummings studies a photo of Cummings himself—a legislative legend. Metropolitan Nashville Government Archives, *Nashville Banner* Collection.

But Preacher Ruffin was her pride and joy. She called on him to say the blessing at the boarding house table.

One Sunday morning, the Unholy Trinity watched from their hotel as Ruffin left the rooming house headed for the penitentiary. They waited a short while, then I. D. Beasley telephoned the rooming house and asked in a sultry woman's voice, "Is Representative Ruffin there?"

"No, he's not here," snapped Miss Clark.

"I wanted to speak to him."

"Well, he's not here."

"When do you expect him back?"

"He'll be back after awhile."

Cummings said that Beasley hung up the phone.

"We all took another drink, and fooled around, and directly I. D. called back in the same woman's voice," Cummings said.

Beasley again got Miss Clark on the phone: "Is Representative Ruffin there?"

"NO!" Miss Clark said. "He's not here. He's out at the—WHO IS THIS?"

Beasley gave her the name of a well-known Nashville prostitute and said, "I'm one of his girlfriends. He asked me to call."

That was too much for Miss Clark: "I want you whores to quit calling here for old Ruffin. He claims to be a preacher and goes out to the prison and preaches all day to those convicts and comes back here and you whores call him."

"Well," Beasley said in the sultry voice, "he's a friend of mine and he asked me to call."

"I'm going to put that old hypocrite out of my rooming house."

Cummings and his co-conspirators watched Ruffin return from the penitentiary about noon and waited expectantly. They did not have to wait long. Soon they saw him coming out carrying two suitcases.

FINDING THE CAPITOL

By tradition, if a bill affected the affairs of only one county, the Tennessee legislature enacted it automatically as a courtesy to that county's legislator. It also was a tradition for the new legislator to take advantage of this courtesy by throwing his enemies out of their government jobs back home. Those jobs then went to the legislator's friends.

An East Tennessee mountaineer got elected and set out for Nashville to fulfill the tradition by abolishing his county's road board. Before the legislature could vote on his proposal, the county road board members appealed to House Speaker Pete Haynes to save their jobs.

Haynes sought to block the mountaineer's bill by trying to befuddle the old man, who, Haynes reasoned, was bound to be timid and scared as he got up before the House of Representatives for the first time. So Haynes asked him about the enacting clause, the caption of the bill, its constitutionality.

Finally, the old mountaineer told him, "Mr. Haynes, I don't know nairy a thing you're talking about, but I do know one thing. These here fellows, they fi't me from one end of the county to the other and they said I was so ignorant that if I got elected I couldn't find the Capitol building. Well, I just want to show them I made it."

The House roared with laughter and Haynes gaveled the bill through.

SPECIAL LICENSE PLATES AND SPOTTED HORSES

As a legislator, not to mention a legend, Jim Cummings was entitled to special license plates for his car. But he rejected such vanity plates.

"I wouldn't have the ———— things," he said. "On my way back and forth to Nashville and other places, occasionally I would stop at places of ill repute, the least of which was bootleggers. When I was in places of questionable conduct, carrying on, I didn't want anybody passing and saying, 'Well, I saw your car at so and so last night.' I never would have one of those ———— things."

Cummings said he learned that lesson early.

"When I was a boy," he said, "there was a young man that lived in our community that had a spotted horse. We all traveled horseback in those days, you know, or we walked a-courtin' or whatever we were doing, moral or immoral. And he had this spotted horse, and everybody knew every ———— place he stopped. Wherever they saw this spotted horse tied, they said, 'Marion, we know where you were last night.' So I got an early lesson in my life not to be identified by your mode of conveyance."

"Mr. Jim" Cummings enjoys a laugh with college students. This photo is believed to have been taken at his beloved Middle Tennessee State University when a dormitory there was named for him. Metropolitan Nashville Government Archives, *Nashville Banner* Collection.

JIM CUMMINGS IN HIS EIGHTIES

When Middle Tennessee State University officials dedicated the dormitory named for Jim Cummings, they invited Cummings, then in his mid-eighties, to visit the young women who lived there. He said: "It reminds me of the girl of the night who happened to get the wrong room number," Cummings told the officials. "She knocked on this fella's door—he was some fella that looked about like me—and she said: 'Pardon me, I knocked on the wrong door.' He said to her, 'No, young lady, you haven't knocked on the wrong door. You're just twenty years too late.'"

Legislative Branch: What Makes You Think They Read the Bills?

In the office of the Speaker of the Tennessee House of Representatives once was a book by a legislator from another state. The book was about that writer's experiences as a legislator. If memory serves correctly, the title was *What Makes You Think We Read the Bills?*

Unfortunately, with thousands of bills and countless amendments being filed during each annual session of the General Assembly, few legislators even attempt to read all the bills. Fortunately, legislative committees dispose of many bills before they get to the floor. Also, lawyers on staff prepare helpful summaries of most legislation. In an earlier time, perhaps legislators could read all the bills and still have time left over. It was this extra time, possibly, that got some legislators into the mischief previously described.

Even today, however, the old expression remains true. There are two things you do not wish to see being made: sausage and laws. The following stories reveal why that is true—at least for laws.

AS IF BACHELORHOOD WERE NOT STRESSFUL ENOUGH

Bachelorhood was put to a severe test in Tennessee in 1826. A bill stringently curtailing the unmarried man's allegedly carefree estate was introduced that year in the General Assembly.

The bill called for a substantial fine to be imposed upon "unmarried men over the age of thirty years, feasting upon the fat of the land; regardless of the claims, which many amiable, worthy and meritorious females have upon our sex for husbands; treating with utter contempt the rites and ceremonies of honorable marriage, thereby, most aggravated by offending against the peace, prosperity, honor, and dignity of the state."

The requested fine was equivalent to 25 percent of a bachelor's estate. At the end of each year, the collected revenue was to be divided among unmarried women of at least twenty-five years of age.

The unfortunate public servant saddled with the responsibility of enforcement was to be the sheriff in each county. If any bachelor unwisely refused to comply when the sheriff came knocking at the door, the legislation prescribed even more dire punishment: "If any man shall be returned by the sheriff a third time for taxation under the provisions of this act, he shall be taken, held and deemed to be an incorrigible bachelor, and shall forever after, until he marries, pay tax of fifty percent on all the estate that he may have; to be collected and paid over, to the same purposes and persons, as is herein before directed."

When brought before the House of Representatives, the bill, according to a note scribbled on the document by Clerk Thomas J. Campbell, was "read one time and passed." Such a quick, supportive decision must have pleased House Clerk Campbell, who was the father of several unmarried daughters.

The Senate, however, as noted by the senate clerk, R. Dance, decisively opposed the proposition. Clerk Dance's remark, scrawled just under Clerk Campbell's, was: "Read and ordered to be laid on the table for 30 years."

No records concerning Clerk Dance's family status are available, so his feelings about the Senate's decision cannot be determined. But Lewis Reneau, the Sevier County lawyer who conceived the bachelor tax bill, had ample cause to champion such legislation: he had four unwed daughters.

SUFFRAGE AND MOTHERHOOD

The fight for nationwide women's suffrage, the right to vote, stretched over at least seventy-two years. The final battleground was in Tennessee.

The Congress approved the Nineteenth Amendment to the United

States Constitution, granting women the right to vote in 1919. Then came the campaign for ratification by three-fourths of the states.

By January 1, 1920, twenty-two states had ratified the constitutional amendment. By the February birthday of women's suffrage leader Susan B. Anthony, ten more states fell in line. In March, Washington was the thirty-fifth state to ratify, leaving just one more state needed. The Suffragists then turned to Tennessee, seeking what cartoonists called the "perfect 36."

Governor Albert Roberts called for an August special session to consider ratification. On the first day of the session, Governor Roberts spoke to the General Assembly and urged ratification to end the "injustice to the womanhood of America."

Suffrage leaders counted their supporters and found the Senate safe, but test votes in the House showed only fifty votes for the cause, the absolute minimum required.

Women of both persuasions greeted and "sweet-talked" legislators. Women gave out flowers to "show their colors." In a "War of the Roses" symbolically reminiscent of the governor's campaign of 1886 between brothers Bob and Alf Taylor, those opposing suffrage wore red roses and those for women's voting wore yellow roses. Some reported bribes, and "ladies of the evening" were being used as persuaders. There were even rumors of kidnappings. At least one legislator was assigned a bodyguard. Governor Roberts was threatened.

The motion to ratify the suffrage amendment passed the Senate by a vote of twenty-five to four. Then the measure came before the House. The Suffragists had counted on twenty-four-year-old Harry T. Burn of Athens, but on the day of the crucial vote Burn showed up wearing a red rose. Proponents were disheartened. Yet, when the vote was taken, to the surprise of nearly everyone, when Burn's name was called, he quickly responded with an "aye."

His vote turned out to be the difference. Tennessee became the crucial thirty-sixth state to ratify the Nineteenth Amendment. Harry Burn was "the man of the hour." But what had changed his mind?

The next day he told the House how it happened. On the morning of the vote, he had received a letter from his mother, Mrs. J. L. Burn of Niota. It read:

Dear Son:

Hurrah, and vote for suffrage! Don't keep them in doubt. I notice some of the speeches against. They were bitter. I have been watching to see how you stood, but have not noticed anything yet. Don't forget to be a good boy and help Mrs. Catt put the "rat" in ratification.

Your Mother

Burns explained his logic to his colleagues: "I know that a mother's advice is always safest for her boy to follow, and my mother wanted me to vote for ratification."

WELCOME TO THE LEGISLATURE

Representative Shelby Rhinehart knew a bill he was sponsoring was in trouble in a committee. He needed another vote, so he approached newly elected Representative Joyce Hassell of Memphis. Like Rhinehart, Representative Hassell was a member of the committee, and she had her very first bill before the committee on that same day.

Representative Rhinehart told the new legislator that she and he both had tough bills up and that they needed to help each other. "If you vote for my bill," Rhinehart told Hassell, "then I'll vote for yours." Hassell thought a moment, then she struck the deal.

Representative Rhinehart's bill came up. Representative Hassell voted for it, and it passed—by one vote.

Representative Hassell's bill came up, but it failed—by one vote. And Representative Rhinehart had voted *against* it.

Representative Hassell was furious. Immediately after the committee meeting, the former teacher hurried over to Rhinehart and jumped him, scolding him as she might have chastised an unruly student. She really let him have it.

When she finally paused to take a breath, Rhinehart grinned and replied: "Welcome to the legislature."

CHAIRMAN BRAGG'S MEETINGS

Representative John Bragg of Murfreesboro was a much-loved member of the legislature who served all but two years between 1965 and 1991. A former newspaper publisher and editor and the owner of a

Legendary House Finance Chair John Bragg (left) hands the ball off to Governor Winfield Dunn. They are standing on the Legislative Plaza and the capitol can be seen behind them. Metropolitan Nashville Government Archives, *Nashville Banner* Collection.

printing company, for many of his twenty-four legislative years he chaired the Finance Ways and Means Committee. This committee always dealt with difficult financial issues, and often the discussions focused on numbers, hardly the most entertaining of subjects. Perhaps because of this, Chairman Bragg often began the committee meetings with a little humor.

For example, one day he began a meeting like this: "Ladies and gentlemen, we have a wonderful audience here and we appreciate you all coming to this meeting. I'd like to see the hand of every married person in this room."

Most everybody raised a hand. Bragg nodded, then said: "I have one bit of advice for you. You forget every mistake you've ever made in life. There's no need of two people keeping up with the same thing all the days of our lives."

At another meeting, Chairman Bragg told about going to his doctor to get his annual checkup. The doctor said: "John, you're gonna have to get in shape."

Chairman Bragg thought about that and responded: "Doctor, round is a shape."

HOUSE JUDICIARY

The House Judiciary Committee historically has been composed primarily of attorneys. Most would agree that lawyers create challenges and can create insurmountable problems. The Judiciary Committee also has been assigned many of the most controversial and technically difficult bills. Furthermore, that committee often gets bills that are politically appealing and thus dangerous to oppose, but which run afoul of obstacles like the constitutions of this state and country.

As a result, the committee meetings often give detailed consideration to proposals that start as better ideas than as legislation. Sometimes the committee will complete work on only a bill or two during a meeting. Once one of us sponsored a bill that enjoyed no less than five weeks of hearings and debate in the committee. You can understand why some legislators have promised that they would leave the legislature before they would serve on the Judiciary Committee.

One recent year near the end of a legislative session, the committee was having extra meetings, as well as extra-long meetings, trying to complete its business. As the committee tried to make up for what was called "the committee's glacial pace at the beginning of the session," the *Tennessee Journal* asked and answered the following question: "Ever wonder what happens to those college students who put off writing term papers until the night before they're due? They're all serving on the House Judiciary Committee. . . ."

JUDICIARY BEANPICKERS

Representative Gary Odom of Nashville once was given a package of frozen green beans in the House Judiciary Committee. The gesture was inspired by reports that Odom had likened the committee to "a truckload of bean pickers in a field without a foreman."

Odom indignantly claimed he was misquoted, saying, "I would never criticize the House Judiciary Committee . . . especially not when I still have bills before them."

BEWLEY'S MOVING BILLS

One of the most beloved legislators in recent years was Representative Joe Bewley. The Greenville Republican loved to laugh and had a gift for making others laugh, too.

One day in the Finance Ways and Means Committee, Representative Bewley was trying to get his bill passed. There was not much support. Bewley himself moved for passage of it, which as a member of the committee he could do. There was a little talk and then the chairman asked if there was a second. When not a member moved to second his bill, Bewley shouted out: "Second!"

Representative Bewley was ruled out of order. But not until everyone had enjoyed a laugh.

MORE BEWLEY MANEUVERING

Representative Bewley was trying to get another bill out of the Finance Ways and Means Committee. He was struggling and had little support. Finally, to end the misery, someone called for a vote. Chairman Bragg called for the ayes and only Bewley's loud but lonely voice was heard. The Chairman called for the nos and everybody else shouted "Nooo!"

Bewley immediately said into the microphone, "I believe the ayes have it."

After the laughter subsided, Chairman Bragg ruled, "The bill passes." And it did.

THE BUCK BEWLEY EXCEPTION

A controversial bill came to the floor of the House of Representatives dealing with lethal injection of animals in local pounds. After two hours of debate, Representative Joe Bewley stood up. He offered an amendment that the legislation not apply to Buck Bewley.

Legislators scratched their heads and attempted to figure out what Representative Dewley was trying to do. Finally, someone stood and asked, "Representative Bewley, may I ask who 'Buck Bewley' is?"

Bewley stood back up and said, "Yes, you may ask. It's my dog."

The House overwhelmingly adopted the Buck Bewley amendment and sent the amended bill to the Senate.

THE LIARS CONTEST—
MORE BEWLEY AND RHINEHART

Representative Bill Richardson of Columbia was awfully proud of his hometown's famous Mule Day Celebration. Of course, Mule Day lasts considerably longer than a day and consists of much more than a huge parade. One of the grandest events is a "Liars Contest." A local civic club sponsors it, and Representative Richardson thought it would impress members of the club if he sponsored a resolution recognizing the Liars Contest.

As Representative Richardson presented his resolution before the House of Representatives, Representative Joe Bewley jumped up and offered an amendment. The amendment was to designate Representative Shelby Rhinehart as the General Assembly's official representative to and contestant in the Liars Contest. There was considerable mirth at the amendment, particularly since some thought it was most appropriate.

Representative Richardson, however, not wanting to have to read or explain the amendment to the local civic club, immediately and vigorously objected.

"Mr. Speaker, Mr. Speaker, this is not right at all! This contest is for *amateurs!*"

REPRESENTATIVE RHINEHART'S
ANNEXATION PROBLEM

Representative Shelby Rhinehart represented Marion County. Within Marion County was a community that feared annexation by nearby Chattanooga. Rhinehart's constituents were quite upset about the prospect of annexation and asked him for help. At the same time, but on the other end of the state, Lieutenant Governor John Wilder represented another community, Hickory Withe, which had a similar fear of annexation.[1]

Representative Rhinehart and Lieutenant Governor Wilder sponsored legislation to protect the two communities they represented and only those two. But that legislation was deemed unconstitutional.

The next year Lieutenant Governor Wilder wanted to try another legislative approach and sent an aide to see whether Representative Rhinehart wanted to try again. Rhinehart, however, did not. He had figured out another and constitutional solution to his problem—and had already taken care of it, unbeknownst to almost anyone except himself.

Marion County is in the central time zone. Chattanooga is on eastern time. Representative Rhinehart had slipped a bill through providing that if a city annexes an area in another county and in another time zone, the annexing city must adopt the time zone of the area being annexed. Rhinehart knew that Chattanooga, population 152,000, would not be so interested in annexing a few hundred people at the expense of changing to the central time zone.

RHINEHART'S REELECTION REFLECTIONS

Representative Shelby Rhinehart was talking to a friend as they walked to the House chamber. It had been a hard day and Rhinehart told his friend: "A person has to be a nut or a real weirdo to do this job."

Then Rhinehart noticed a grinning reporter within earshot.

Representative Shelby Rhinehart stands pointing for affirmative votes while his friend Representative Gene Davidson expresses his request for negative votes. Rhinehart is the long-time chair of the infamous "Black Hole Subcommittee" (so named because bills going into the Revenues and Expenditures Subcommittee often disappear, never to be seen again). For related reasons, Rhinehart is known as the "Prince of Darkness," but he is also notable for his effectiveness and his quick replies and actions. Metropolitan Nashville Government Archives, *Nashville Banner* Collection.

Rhinehart quickly asked the reporter: "Please don't quote me—I'm running for reelection."

This is the same legislator that once told a crowd: "All that would like to contribute to my campaign, please rise."

Then immediately had the band play the national anthem.

REPRESENTATIVE RHINEHART'S BODYGUARD

For many years, Representative Shelby Rhinehart chaired the Revenues and Expenditure Subcommittee. It was the subcommittee of the Finance Ways and Means Committee where all legislation involving substantial amounts of money had to go. It also was known as the "Black Hole Subcommittee" because bills assigned to it often disappeared as though into a Black Hole.

Representative Rhinehart ran the Black Hole Subcommittee with an iron hand. Many a legislator came in and could not even get a motion to move his or her bill out. Representative Rhinehart was known to kill as many as seven bills with one quick-gaveled ruling. Such tactics inspired some strong feelings and created some passionate foes.

One time Representative Rhinehart was on his way to a Black Hole Subcommittee meeting when he spotted Representative Charles Curtiss, a freshman legislator but, more importantly, a real physical specimen. Representative Rhinehart invited the former Marine to come with him to the Black Hole Subcommittee, explaining, "We're expecting that there may be some trouble."

Representative Curtiss, never one to back away from a fight, replied: "Mr. Chairman, I can't keep them from cussin' you, but they will never lay a hand on you."

BEER AND DYNAMITE

The captions of bills are supposed to disclose what the bills are about. But that does not mean the captions always disclose what legislators really intend to do with the bills. That has been demonstrated on numerous occasions, but perhaps the best example involved the issue of whether Guinness beer could be sold in kegs in Tennessee.

State law is specific about the size of kegs that can be sold, and Guinness, a beer imported from Ireland, is placed in metric kegs that did not fit Tennessee's legal parameters. A bill to allow Guinness beer to be sold in the metric kegs passed the Senate but failed in the House. Representative Mike Kernell of Memphis, who supported allowing Guinness to use metric kegs, was determined not to be stopped. The next year he sought to allow metric kegs by amending a bill that originally had nothing to do with the sale of beer by the keg. What was that bill he amended originally about? It was a bill to regulate the use of dynamite.

BURNETT AND NEW UNDERSTANDINGS

For many years K. C. Dodson was a lobbyist for the Tennessee Farm Bureau Federation. He often worked closely with Representative Tommy Burnett, who represented hundreds of farmers on the Upper Cumberland. One day Dodson learned Burnett was sponsoring a bill that the Farm Bureau very much opposed. The veteran lobbyist went to see Representative Burnett.

"Tommy, I want you to handle this bill in such a manner that I can take you by the hand and lead you to those 847 Farm Bureau members in your district. I'd like to be able to tell them how you have helped us and been with us. I'd like to be able to tell them how good you are to work with us and to work for them. I'd like to be able to, but this bill you're sponsoring. . . ." With that Dodson stopped, looked sadly at Tommy, and shook his head.

Representative Burnett looked him in the eyes and said, "Well, Mr. Dodson, I've never had that bill explained to me that way. It may be my bill, but I don't think it ought to pass."

MOVING BILLS

Representative Joe Armstrong once offered an amendment to his own bill. He explained the amendment to the Health and Human Resources Committee this way: "The amendment merely rewrites the bill."

Another frequent non-explanation of a bill is this one: "The bill does exactly what the caption says."

When the sponsor says only that, legislators scramble through their piles of bills and other documents, trying to read the caption. Often the bill has been voted on and is gone before everyone can read the caption and know what the bill does.

THE EXPLODING MICROPHONE

C. E. DePriest was a representative from Giles County. The farmer and World War II veteran served in the House for eighteen years. His 1990 defeat came during a raging controversy over a hazardous waste incinerator proposed for his home county. Later he observed, "I was the first person that got incinerated in this toxic waste incinerator deal here."

As one of Representative DePriest's last sessions drew to a close, the representatives were getting a little cranky. They were considering dozens of bills at a furious pace, then having to wait for the Senate to confirm the House's actions or send the bills back. As they waited, some of Representative DePriest's colleagues began looking for entertainment.

Before speaking, Representative DePriest always blew into his microphone to see if it was on. He never spoke into it or tapped it, as others did; he just blew. It was a unique habit that amused his colleagues.

On this particular day, the manufacturers of Dr. Scholl's Foot Powder had given each legislator a sample of their fine foot powder. As one of DePriest's colleagues looked at his container of foot powder, he thought how funny it would be to unscrew the top of DePriest's microphone and fill it with foot powder.

When the Speaker declared a recess, DePriest took the opportunity to go to the rest room. His mischievous colleague took advantage of his absence to unscrew the top of his microphone and fill it with the foot powder.

DePriest had been speaking before the recess, so he was expected to resume speaking when the House again was called to order. Thus, with television cameras rolling, a gallery full of visitors, and ninety-eight other representatives knowing what was going to happen and trying hard not to laugh too soon, C. E. DePriest took up his microphone. As always he blew, and when he huffed, the foot powder exploded out. The white powder flew into his face and everywhere around him. It coated his glasses, covered his face, and hung on his eyebrows.

Representative DePriest stood there as the dust literally settled. Finally, he took his glasses off, leaving his eyes looking like two dark holes in a white bank of snow. Then he simply said: "I hope whoever did this has splinters run up their fingernails."

CASKET LEGISLATION COMES ALIVE IN HOUSE DEBATE

"Would you buy a used casket from this man?"

That was the question asked after the House passed and sent to the Senate legislation that would allow funeral directors to rent or sell the outer shells of previously used caskets.

Representative Tim Garrett of Nashville, a funeral director and sponsor of the bill, said the legislation dealt only with caskets that have been used for traditional services in which the body is later removed and cremated or donated to science.

The bill generated the expected spate of gallows humor.

"Would these caskets be rented by the day or by the hour?" asked Representative Larry Turner of Memphis.

"I see a lot of rent-to-own furniture," observed Representative Steve McDaniel of Lexington. "Do you rent to own or how does this work?"

"Just rent," Garrett replied.

BANKING AND COCKFIGHTING

In 1989, East Tennessean Ralph Cole first ran for the legislature. Early in his campaign, he walked into the office of the president of a bank and introduced himself. He explained that he was running for state representative and would appreciate the bank president's support. Sitting behind the big, fine desk and without cracking a smile, the banker immediately asked Cole how he felt about cockfighting.

Cole recalls that he didn't know "whether to fall through the floor or jump out a window" because here was the president of a bank asking him about rooster fighting. Cole finally blurted out that he didn't have any feelings one way or another, but added that when he was a youngster he had gone to some cockfights with his uncle.

It turned out that the president of the bank was a strong supporter of cockfighting. Cole's answer must have satisfied him since he became one of Representative Cole's most loyal supporters and advisors.

REPRESENTATIVE YARD BOY

Right after Representative Mike Williams was elected in a very close vote, a woman from the small community of Pegram called him. She was terribly upset over weeds that had grown up in the right-of-way of a state road. Representative Williams listened attentively to her, his attentiveness enhanced by the narrowness of his recent victory. He assured her that he would take care of the weeds and went to work.

Representative Williams called Commissioner of Transportation Jimmy Evans, who told Representative Williams, "We'll get to them." But Representative Williams could tell that he had not exactly established the new top priority for the Department of Transportation. Deciding not to risk making the woman angrier, he borrowed a lawn mower, drove to Pegram, and found the woman's house. He got the push mower out of his vehicle, then himself proceeded to mow all of the right-of-way anywhere near her house.

Williams then drove back to Franklin, returned the lawn mower, went home, showered, and called the woman. He was eager to receive praise for his extraordinary actions, but he restrained himself, merely asking if the right-of-way looked better now. The response was quick.

"You need to get some physical fitness programs for these state employees. That fat boy that was out here, I thought he was going to sweat himself into a heart attack!"

Representative Williams never could bring himself to tell the woman that he had been the "fat boy." Instead he just listened to the constituent complain some more, then told her he appreciated her having called.

DALE ALLEN AND THE NEWSPAPER PHOTO

Around 1990, the Memphis *Commercial Appeal* was researching a story on what legislators do in Nashville when not legislating. When the reporter asked me what I (Roy Herron) did, I told him that I enjoy running. The reporter asked whether he could go along—in a car. We arranged to meet at Nashville's downtown YMCA at 5:30 the next morning.

Then the reporter called back. He said it would be dark at 5:30 A.M., which I acknowledged. The reporter, however, said he wanted a photograph. So we rescheduled our meeting for later.

The next morning at 6:00 A.M., the reporter and a photographer were at the YMCA. Dale Allen, a native of northwest Tennessee whom I have known since college, and I went for our usual run. The reporter and photographer followed in the car.

Dale and I wound up in a color photo on the front of a section of the Sunday paper. I brought the paper back to Nashville on Monday and gave it to Dale, who in addition to being an attorney is a lobbyist. I told him, "Now I can't vote for any more of your bills."

Dale thought about that a second and replied, "When the heck did you ever vote for any of my bills any way?"

WORK OF TWO MEN

State Representative Ronnie Cole of Dyersburg was the master of ceremonies at the retirement dinner for Brad Miller, a veteran road builder and the lobbyist and executive director of the Tennessee Road Builders Association. Representative Cole, a road builder himself, said of his long-time friend: "Brad Miller has done the work of *two* men."

Pause.

"Frank and Jesse James."

EARLY BIRDS AND EARLY WORMS

Representatives Paul Phelan and Ronnie Cole were elected to the legislature at the same time. They roomed together at the Hermitage Hotel, sharing a suite. Some mornings, Representative Cole would rise only to find his roommate had not. He then loudly challenged his roommate to face the new day.

One morning after Representative Phelan had been out late entertaining constituents from home, Representative Cole woke him earlier than he wanted. Representative Phelan finally responded to Representative Cole's admonitions that the early bird gets the worm.

"Cole, you know what your problem is?" Representative Phelan asked.

Representative Cole allowed as how he did not know.

"You spend too much time worrying about the good luck of the early *bird*, without spending enough time thinking about the bad luck of the early *worm*."

TOUCHDOWNS AND PAPERWADS

Students from a high school in my district were attending a floor session of the House of Representatives. From the balcony they watched the proceedings. On the floor I (Roy Herron) noticed a student holding his arms above his head. I wondered if the student was waving at another legislator on the floor, but no one seemed to be waving back.

I looked again and the student had his arms raised again, as if he were a football referee signaling a touchdown. I kept looking at the student and could not figure out what in the world he was doing. The student was behind a stone column where the Speaker could not see him, but others certainly could.

I looked around again and finally saw, on the far side of the chamber, one of my colleagues trying to shoot a paperwad across the "goal posts" the student formed with his arms. I told him that the "goal posts" belonged to one of my constituents. I thought he would say, "Well, I don't mean to get the boy in trouble or anything." Or maybe he even would offer some sort of apology.

Instead, he said, "Well, I had a rubber band here that would do it, but it broke on me. Otherwise I could shoot it across there."

Undaunted, however, he kept on firing away.

This was the same day that the Speaker of the Australian House of Representatives was visiting and sat in the back of the chamber. My colleague missed the goal posts, but he did not miss the Australian Speaker.

REPRESENTATIVE RINKS'S INTRODUCTION

Representative Randy Rinks once gave a glowing introduction to a speaker. The speaker walked to the podium and said, "Well, that introduction is kind of like perfume. You can smell it, but don't swallow it."

The speaker said some nice things about Representative Rinks, then added, "And I hear that Representative Rinks is a self-made man."

Rinks's wife, Sherry, immediately elbowed her beloved and brought Rinks back down to earth, whispering: "That relieves the Lord of a great responsibility."

THE TWILIGHT ZONE

Lieutenant Governor Wilder tells of going away on a trip. Before he left, he instructed his administrative assistant to get the ceiling in his legislative office lowered. He also had asked for some less harsh lighting. When he got back his office was as it is now: low ceiling, recessed lighting, dark with shadows.

Mayor Dick Hackett of Memphis came to visit him in the dark office. When they finished, Wilder walked Mayor Hackett out into the well-lit hallway. At which point Mayor Hackett said to Governor Wilder: "I'm glad we came out here. You've been in *The Twilight Zone.*"

WILDER AND THE PREACHER LOBBYIST

Lieutenant Governor John Wilder once encountered an especially thorny issue on which he was going to have to vote. The main lobbyist for the bill was also a preacher. The preaching lobbyist told Wilder that he had talked with the Lord and the Lord wanted Wilder to vote for the bill.

Wilder thought about that a while then told the lobbyist-preacher that he also had a good relationship with the Lord and that "if He wants me to vote for it, the Lord should speak to me directly."

Lieutenant Governor John Wilder (left), House Speaker Ned McWherter (center), and Governor Lamar Alexander (right) share a laugh before Governor Alexander delivers his budget address on February 2, 1981. Metropolitan Nashville Government Archives, *Nashville Banner* Collection.

SPEAKER MCWHERTER FLYING
WITH SPEAKER WILDER

When Ned McWherter was Speaker of the House of Representatives and John Wilder was Speaker of the Senate, during election years they would travel the state together, helping elect members to their respective bodies.

Once they were in Knoxville, campaigning for legislative candidates and attending a Democratic rally. Speaker Wilder had flown McWherter there in Wilder's plane. As they were about to return to West Tennessee, Josie Burson from Memphis asked if she could hitch a ride. Of course, they graciously consented.

At the airport, Wilder was calculating how much fuel he could load in his small plane and still carry his two passengers and their luggage. He asked McWherter his weight, which McWherter replied was 245 pounds. Wilder did the math, then fueled the plane accordingly. Then their friend showed up with a big suitcase. Speaker Wilder took it, strained to carry it, then struggled to lift and put it in the small plane. Speaker McWherter carefully watched Wilder, then slowly walked over to him.

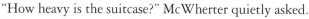

"How heavy is the suitcase?" McWherter quietly asked.

"Heavy," Wilder replied.

"Real heavy?" McWherter asked.

"Real heavy!" Wilder replied.

McWherter thought a second, then blurted his confession: "I need to tell you, John, I lied about my weight. I don't weigh 245, I weigh 275."

A PRESIDENT AS RECEPTIONIST
FOR SPEAKER MCWHERTER

When former Georgia governor Jimmy Carter ran for president, the campaign started out small and cheap. When he visited Tennessee, Carter and his press secretary, Jody Powell, would fly commercial to Nashville. Sometimes Larry Daughtrey, the *Nashville Tennessean* political reporter, would pick them up at the airport. By the time he brought them downtown, he would have the latest information on the campaign.

Usually Carter and Powell would go to Speaker Ned McWherter's office and visit and hang out there. Carter and McWherter were close, and McWherter and his top aide, House Chief Clerk Jim Free, were early and strong supporters of Carter. In fact, Free left McWherter's staff to go to work in the Carter White House.

After Carter, Powell and Free were in the White House, one day Larry Daughtrey needed some information from Powell, now the president's press secretary. Powell did not call Daughtrey back, so Daughtrey called again. And again. Finally, nearing a deadline, needing the information, and feeling like Powell had forgotten his old friend, Daughtrey called the White House and left a message for President Carter: "Mr. President, please have Jody Powell call me. Larry."

In a matter of moments Powell called back: "Did you need me?"

Not long after that, Daughtrey told Speaker McWherter the story of what he had done to get Powell's call. McWherter chuckled, then he got serious. "That darn Jim Free won't call me back either. I bet if I left a message for President Carter to have him call me, somebody'd get hold of Free and he'd call me back then. I'm going to keep that in mind the next time I need him."

A few days later, Speaker McWherter needed to talk to Free. He called, but Free did not return McWherter's call. McWherter then called the White House again and said he'd like to leave a message for President Carter. The operator put him on hold and in a few seconds a familiar south Georgia voice came on the line: "Ned, this is Jimmy. What can I do for you?"

The stunned McWherter stammered a moment, then said: "Mr. President, could you get Jim Free to call me?"

SAM DONALDSON AND THE HILLBILLY SPEAKER

When Jimmy Carter was president, Speaker Ned McWherter was at the White House for a meeting. Sam Donaldson of ABC News came rushing along, as he usually does. He bumped into McWherter, literally. He immediately and tactfully said something like: "Get out of the way, you fat hillbilly!"

And Donaldson went on his hurried way.

Some time later President Carter came to Tennessee. During his visit, Carter was about to address a joint session of the General Assembly in the Capitol's House Chamber. Donaldson, still covering the White House, was along on the trip. Just before Carter was to speak, Donaldson came surging along, about to enter the House chamber. As he started to go through the huge doors at the rear of the chamber, he was met by the large presence of McWherter's sergeant at arms, Greg O'Rear, who stepped directly in his path.

"Get out of my way," Donaldson angrily said, "I'm Sam Donaldson with ABC."

"No, sir, you're not allowed in here," O'Rear firmly replied. And Donaldson wasn't.

As Donaldson sat in the lobby outside the House Chamber during Carter's speech, he finally figured out who the "fat hillbilly" was.

CHAIRMAN COOPER

Senator Jerry Cooper, chair of the Senate Commerce Committee, ran for the United States Congress in the middle of his state senate term. That meant that even if he lost, he still would be in the state senate.

Cooper and friends joked: "What do you call a defeated congressional candidate?"

Answer: "Mr. Chairman."

It was funnier to some than to the lobbyists who had bills they knew would go to Commerce Committee. They knew Cooper would chair the committee even if he lost the congressional race. And so they felt a need to contribute accordingly.

When important health care legislation Senator Cooper was sponsoring was narrowly defeated, someone put up signs in the legislative hallways declaring the bill dead and suggesting that memorials could be sent to "Cooper for Congress."

LIEUTENANT GOVERNOR FRANK GORRELL'S TICK JOHNSON

Tennessee's former Lieutenant Governor Frank Gorrell grew up in Logan County, Kentucky. He liked to tell the story of another native of his home county.

Tick Johnson was a perennial candidate for sheriff of Logan County. He ran many times, but never came close to his heart's desire. When

Former Lieutenant Governor Frank Gorrell and Governor Lamar Alexander share a laugh—and about four dollars. Metropolitan Nashville Government Archives, *Nashville Banner* Collection.

the Spanish-American War came along, he saw his opportunity to become a war hero—and sheriff of Logan County. He volunteered and soon became one of the least rough of Teddy Roosevelt's Rough Riders.

At the now famous Battle of San Juan Hill, the fighting was fierce. Tick soon found himself pinned down behind a large rock. As he hunkered down, he wondered whether he'd ever again see the bluegrass of home. Suddenly he heard someone behind him, turned, and saw Colonel Teddy Roosevelt himself.

"This is a great and momentous occasion," the colonel shouted to Tick. "You see those guns up there?" Roosevelt demanded, pointing up the hill to the blazing Spanish guns whose projectiles Tick also had seen. Tick nodded. Roosevelt passionately declared: "The man who leads us up there," Roosevelt urged Tick, "can be the next President of the United States."

Tick thought a moment and replied: "That's okay, Colonel Roosevelt, you go ahead. All I want to be is sheriff of Logan County."

SENATOR ROCHELLE'S TEDDY ROOSEVELT STORY

Senator Bob Rochelle tells the story of when Teddy Roosevelt was about to end his service in the White House. At that time, the rugged outdoorsman began planning a big game hunting trip to Africa. President Roosevelt invited a renowned hunter with special expertise in African big game hunting to visit and teach him at the White House. On the appointed day, the expert arrived and went into the Oval Office to see the president. Two hours later, the expert came out.

One of the White House staffers, surprised by the length of the visit and curious about the conversation, asked the expert: "What did you tell the President?"

The expert quickly replied: "My name. After that, he did all the talking."

SENATOR WOMACK'S DAUGHTER'S PHONE CALL

Everybody who has held elected office probably has a "phone story." Not long after Senator Andy Womack of Murfreesboro had been elected, an irate constituent called his home. When told by Senator

Womack's daughter that he was not there, the constituent apparently thought the daughter was Womack's wife.

The caller lit in on the daughter, denouncing some terrible travesty that Senator Womack allegedly had committed. After listening to a considerable amount of invective against her father, the teenager tried to disengage herself from the conversation. The constituent was having none of that and continued to rant and rave.

Finally, the youngster had listened to all the attacks upon her father she could stand. She again tried politely to end the conversation, but when she could not, she decided to hang up. And she did. But not until after she said: "Eat a booger!"

WHOSE FRIEND?

Commissioner of Conservation and Environment Milton Hamilton previously served as a senator in the General Assembly with Representatives John Tanner, Jimmy Naifeh, and Clyde Webb. One evening the four of them left a legislative reception and wound up going out to Richland Country Club together along with another fellow. They all rode together and were visiting and having a large time. Each legislator assumed the fifth fellow was a friend of his colleagues.

At the country club, one legislator finally asked another, "Who's your friend?"

Which drew the response: "He's not *my* friend. I thought he was *your* friend."

Soon all four legislators discovered that none of them had any idea who the fifth fellow was. When they asked the fellow, they learned he was a furniture salesman from Chattanooga. The gentleman explained: "You all were having such a good time, I just thought I'd join you!"

DUCKS AND GATORS

A petroleum company wanted House Speaker Ned McWherter and Senator Milton Hamilton to fly down and look at their oil rigs in Louisiana. After they had looked at the oil rigs, they went to hunt ducks at a fine place the company had for their corporate executives and guests.

A Cajun fellow poled them out through the marshes in a pirogue. Then he left them in the blind where they were to hunt, explaining that he would be back later in the day to pick them up.

Soon they heard a lot of water thrashing, but were not sure what caused that sound. They discovered the source after they shot a duck and it fell into the water. An alligator leaped from right underneath them and went and got the duck.

They shot ten ducks that day—and the alligator ate three of them.

SPEAKING HERE TONIGHT

One Thursday night I (Roy Herron) spoke to a group of teachers in Union City.

The next day, Friday, at lunch I spoke at the Union City Rotary Club. There I saw a very nice woman whom I also had seen the night before.

The next evening, Saturday, I went to an appreciation dinner for my U.S. congressman, John Tanner. There again was the same woman who also had been at the two events the two previous days when I had spoken.

When I saw her for the third straight day, she looked at me with a pretty smile but the eyes of a deer looking into headlights. As I shook her hand, it was almost limp and she barely could talk as she begged, "You're not speaking here tonight also, are you?"

I paused, then admitted, "Ma'am, I'm afraid I am."

I thought I was going to have to call 9-1-1.

Trying to change the subject as quickly as I could, I asked where she went to church.

With an agonized look, she quickly pleaded, "You're not preaching there tomorrow, are you!?"

THE BLACK POODLE HAT

Chairman John Bragg sought the attention of the full House and gallery in the chamber of the House of Representatives. Finally, Chairman Bragg got the Speaker's recognition, and he said: "Mr. Speaker, somebody has brought me a pair of socks and a hat that they left at Printer's Alley last night. I think it was found by a show girl at the Black Poodle. If anybody knows whose socks and hat this is, please let me know."

As he lifted the socks and hat high, everyone in the House instantly recognized Chairman Rob Robinson's unique hat.

The Speaker began hollering, "Order! Order! Order in the House!"

Of course, Chairman John Bragg had stolen Chairman Robinson's hat and was up to another prank.

Executive Branch:
Governors and the Ungovernable

Tennessee has had a long line of distinguished governors, as well as a few that we might best honor by learning from their mistakes. But there are reasons why it is called the art of governing and not the science of governing. Following is some of the most humorous art created by Tennessee's governors in the twentieth century.

GOVERNOR HOOPER'S PAST—
AND TENNESSEE'S FUTURE

Ben Hooper ran for governor in 1910. As he later wrote, "The campaign had not progressed very far until opposition newspapers began to make occasional reference to my birth and early history." Hooper's mother had not been married when he was conceived and born. Though he later was adopted by his father, the circumstances of his birth were thought particularly scandalous at the time.

At first during the campaign, Hooper ignored the references, but finally he had to respond. He did so in a single dismissive sentence: "The people of Tennessee are not so greatly concerned about where I came from, as they are about where I am going and what I will do there."

Apparently he was right. He was elected.

GOVERNOR HOOPER ON GOVERNOR PATTERSON

Governor Ben Hooper once criticized a predecessor, saying, "Governor Patterson was eminently fitted for the performance of such a task, but at that period of his life he must have been like the horse-jockey's blind mule that butted his head against the barn, which performance the jockey explained by saying that the mule wasn't blind—he just didn't give a ———."

GOVERNOR HOOPER'S BOY

When Ben Hooper's time as governor was over, he and his family headed back to East Tennessee. The conductor on their train, who knew very well who Hooper's little boy Randolph was, wanted to make conversation with the little boy. The conductor asked, "Sonny, whose boy are you?"

Randolph Hooper replied, "I used to be Governor Hooper's boy."

GOVERNOR BROWNING AND THE PHILIPPINES

Gordon Browning was a congressman for a dozen years and Tennessee's governor for six years and finally involuntarily retired from office in 1953. A former military officer and World War I hero, Browning told this favorite story of a political campaign after another war.

It seems a constable decided it was time to move up, so he announced for Congress.

The constable traveled all over West Tennessee talking about sin and corruption and what he was going to do about it if elected to Congress.

This was just after the Spanish-American War, and the country was full of talk about what to do with the Philippines. One Saturday as the constable made his stock speech on a court square, someone in the crowd yelled: "What about the Philippines?"

The candidate ignored the question and continued his diatribe.

But again the man yelled: "What about the Philippines?"

Again the constable ignored the heckler and continued, but a third time the man yelled, this time even more insistently: "What about the Philippines?"

The constable stopped, scratched his head, and replied: "Best I recollect, the Apostle Paul wrote them fellers a letter nearly 2,000 years ago and they ain't never answered yet. If they can't show the Apostle no more respect than that, I ain't a-gonna worry 'bout no Philippines."

GORDON BROWNING AND ALVIN YORK

Tennessee hero and Congressional Medal of Honor winner Alvin York of Pall Mall and his fellow World War I veteran Gordon Browning were great friends. During one of Gordon Browning's three races for reelection as governor, he was headed to speak at the court square in York's home county of Fentress. As Browning came past York's home, he saw York standing by the road. Browning stopped the car to see his good friend. York, it turned out, had been there for a purpose.

York said he had been standing there beside the road just to warn Browning of something. York told Browning there were three bad fellows at the courthouse in Jamestown who had sworn to kill Browning if he spoke. York said he believed that they not only intended to kill Browning, but in fact would do so if he went ahead and tried to speak there.

Browning, who himself did not lack for courage, told York that the Governor of Tennessee could not be intimidated like that.

York tried every way he knew to persuade Browning not to go ahead, but Browning refused to turn away.

Finally, York told Browning that if he insisted, then he should give York a fifteen minute head start in getting to town. Browning reluctantly agreed, York headed for Jamestown, then Browning followed fifteen minutes later.

When Browning got to the courthouse, he went to where the crowd eagerly awaited him. There were, however, three empty seats on the front row.

After Browning spoke without incident, his friend York explained, lifting his coat jacket to reveal a pistol on his hip: "I told the three that if even one of them blinked, I would kill them all three. And they decided to go on."

GORDON BROWNING AND HIS BRIDE

The late Gordon Browning (1895–1976) of Carroll County was an attorney, a veteran of World War I, and still in his twenties when he was elected to the first of six terms in Congress. Much later he told the story about the night his wife "just refused to attend some social function we had been invited to and I accused her of being a terrible wife for a congressman to have." Browning said his wife fired right back: "That's all right, Sonny. . . . I'll be a mighty fine wife to settle down with after you get beat!"[1]

In 1934, Congressman Browning ran for the U.S. Senate and, sure enough, he was beaten. Browning, however, was not interested in his wife's suggestion he "settle down" after his defeat. Instead, in 1936 he ran for governor and won.

During World War II, Browning served in various positions. In January 1946, Lieutenant Colonel Browning was assigned to Germany and was made director of military government in the Bremen Enclave. His position carried with it much responsibility but provided much luxury. He tried to get his wife to join him in Germany, but again she put him in his place. Browning told it this way: "I told her about the big house and servants and other comforts but she wouldn't come. She just said I had better make well of it because I wouldn't have it that good much more."[2]

After the war, Browning served as governor again, winning elections in 1948 and 1950 before being defeated by Frank Clement in 1952. Then Browning, having finished his public service, bought considerable stock in a life insurance company in Jackson, Tennessee. He became chairman of the board of directors. For a decade, he daily drove seventy miles between his home in Huntingdon and his office in Jackson. When asked why he did not move to Jackson to be near his office, he again noted his wife's independence. He explained that he had "married a Huntingdon girl. She just won't go. And I'm too old to start living alone—or to organize another woman."[3]

GOVERNOR CLEMENT'S PUBLIC SPEAKING

Frank Clement the youth was as aggressive in love as Clement the man was in politics. Pushing his luck relentlessly, he gradually hunted down all the pictures of his sweetheart that other young men had collected and talked them away from their owners. He urged his girlfriend to marry him when they were sixteen; she refused, so he asked again when they were seventeen; after she refused again, he repeated himself when they were eighteen.

Governor Clement once said that his first experience in public speaking came when he put his proposals to Lucille over a party-line telephone.

Governor Frank Clement appears to be hitchhiking on the new Interstate 40 that runs east-west across Tennessee. Senator Albert Gore Sr. was known as the "father of the interstate highways" and worked with President Dwight Eisenhower in the 1950s to make the interstate system a reality. Metropolitan Nashville Government Archives, *Nashville Banner* Collection.

GOVERNOR CLEMENT'S ORATORY

Clement's own rise to power, as he himself candidly recognized, was due to his oratory. His other remarkable abilities never would have obtained for him the eminence which his speech captured for him.

"I knew I shouldn't have come here," a listener once said. "I was against him all summer, and now he's sold me all over again."

GOVERNOR CLEMENT AND ROADS

Governor Frank Clement revealed not only his knowledge of geography and history, but also his expertise in elections when he said:

> The highest road in the world is in the Andes.
> The oldest road in the world is the Appian Way.
> But the most important road in the world is the one by my house.

TENNESSEE COLONELS

When Frank Clement became governor, he began naming "Tennessee Colonels." The certificates were pretty, the title important-sounding, the meaning dubious. Still, people wanted to know: "How on earth do you get to become a Tennessee Colonel?"

Asked one candid candidate: "I play the Tennessee Waltz every Sunday night on the piano for Mr. Hanky of the Marietta Eagles Club. . . . Is that enough qualifications?"

GOVERNOR CLEMENT AND MOUNTAIN CITY

This story is told of Frank Clement's campaigning for reelection as governor of Tennessee back in the 1950s. In those days, winning the Democratic nomination essentially was winning the election. And that meant Clement had to campaign hard during the heat of the summer before the August primary.

One terribly hot day Clement had to go to Mountain City, a small community in extreme northeast Tennessee. The town was perhaps most famous for being so inaccessible.

As Clement's driver tried to make them less late, he drove as quickly as he dared up the narrow, winding, torturous road through the mountains to Mountain City. As they careened up the mountain in the un-air-conditioned car, the combination of heat, turns, and stress made Clement carsick. In fact, very carsick.

But eventually, when all occupants of the car thought they were going to lose either their lunch or their lives, they arrived in Mountain City. To their amazement, they found a huge crowd had assembled to hear Governor Clement.

It was an extraordinary crowd for such a small, rural, remote place. And it was particularly extraordinary since it was right in the most Republican area of the state. As he surveyed the large crowd, Governor Clement started feeling better. He buttoned his shirt, tightened his tie, and even pulled on his suit coat.

Clement waded through the crowd and shook hands and hugged and kissed his way to the flatbed trailer from which he was to speak. By the time he mounted that trailer, he was feeling much better.

Governor Clement began speaking to the people in his eloquent way. His handsome appearance, passionate oratory, and the substance of what he said moved the people.

Governor Clement told the crowd what he would do for the elderly if they would only give him the opportunity.

Governor Buford Ellington (left) and Governor Frank Clement served together and "leap frogged" each other in the 1950s and 1960s. Metropolitan Nashville Government Archives, *Nashville Banner* Collection.

He told the working people what he would do for them if they would only work for him.

He told the young people what he would do for them if they would only encourage their parents and their neighbors to help him help them.

Finally, caught up in his own rhetoric and the crowd's cheers, he concluded his remarks with this passionate promise: "And ladies and gentlemen, if you will but again elect me your governor, then the next time I come to Mountain City, I will be riding a four-lane highway right straight up the side of this mountain!"

The listeners, all of whom had suffered similar bouts of illness traveling that crooked road, could not believe their ears. For a moment they stood in stunned silence, then the crowd went absolutely wild.

Older citizens wept.

The middle-aged applauded and cheered and whistled wildly.

Young parents hoisted their youngsters up on their shoulders and held them over their heads to see this great governor who was going to build them this great highway.

Some said that even the dogs howled, and the cats purred.

And with that rhetorical flourish, Governor Clement descended from the truck-trailer, waded back through the crowd, got into his car, and began the descent down the same awful, narrow, winding road.

Very quickly, Governor Clement became carsick again. He pulled off his coat. He loosened his tie. He unbuttoned his shirt. And his head sank to the seat.

But his young aide was so disturbed he could not let Governor Clement rest. And so up he spoke: "Governor Clement, you know how much I believe in you. You know how I trust you. You know how I admire you. But I must say that I am most troubled by what I heard you say."

Governor Clement opened one eye partially and replied: "Well, Johnny, what is it that bothers you so?"

Johnny responded: "Governor, you know how much I believe in you, your integrity and honesty, you keeping your promises. But today, Governor, for the very first time since I've known you, you made a promise you simply cannot keep."

"Johnny, whatever do you mean?"

"Governor Clement, I doubt any highway, much less a four-lane highway, could be built straight up the side of this mountain. But even if it could, to do so would bankrupt the state! And now you have promised those people that highway and for the life of me I don't see how you can keep that promise."

Even in his misery, Clement smiled, and he quietly replied: "Johnny, my son, you were not listening closely enough. I never told those people I was going to build them a highway. I simply said before I ever went back to that forsaken place, there would have to be such a highway."[4]

BUFORD ELLINGTON AND DRUE SMITH

Today, many know Drue Smith as the most flamboyant dresser in the Capitol Hill press corps. In the 1950s, however, she was the receptionist in the Cordell Hull State Office Building in Nashville. At that time of few state office buildings, she was in the key place to see everyone coming to do business with, seek help from, or work with state government. When people came into the building, she directed them to whatever office they needed to visit. That meant she knew everyone, knew whom they were going to see, and often knew a great deal about their business. It was a job that she greatly enjoyed.

During the years in which Frank Clement and Buford Ellington

The legendary Drue Smith, state worker, political activist, and journalist, gets ready to record Governor Ray Blanton.

were "leap frogging" as governor, Drue Smith got along extremely well with Governor Clement. But at some point when Buford Ellington was governor, she and he had a falling out, and he fired her. She not only lost her employment, but also her opportunity to know everyone and everything. It was a bitter blow.

In 1972 when Buford Ellington died, his body "lay in state" while mourners came to pay their respects. Shortly before the funeral service was about to begin, despite their past differences and bitter feelings, one of the mourners who came down the aisle was Drue Smith.

A long line of mourners slowly walked past the open casket, gazing upon Governor Ellington's body. When Drue Smith finally paused in front of the casket, she not only looked upon Governor Ellington, but, according to the story, she reached out and grabbed his cheek between her forefinger and thumb and pinched.

"Drue!" exclaimed the person in line next to her, "What are you doing?"

Drue finally turned loose of Governor Ellington's cheek. She explained, "I just wanted to make sure the rascal was really dead."

Governor Buford Ellington served as commissioner of agriculture under Governor Clement, managed Clement's campaign, and "leap-frogged" with him in the executive residence. Here, he looks as if he has had enough shoveling. Metropolitan Nashville Government Archives, *Nashville Banner* Collection.

Governor Ellington (right), after serving in Washington in the administration of his good friend President Lyndon B. Johnson, moved from a conservative or relatively reactionary position on issues of racial equality to more moderate or progressive views. Tennessee did not suffer the extent of violence and lawlessness that some other states suffered. Much of the credit, of course, goes to the people of Tennessee, but considerable recognition should also be given to Ellington, Governor Clement, and U.S. Senators Estes Kefauver, Albert Gore Sr., and Howard Baker. Metropolitan Nashville Government Archives, *Nashville Banner* Collection.

GOVERNOR ALEXANDER, PRESIDENT REAGAN, AND SPEAKER MCWHERTER'S FENCING

A presidential visit is an exciting event. So, it was understandable that Governor Lamar Alexander's administration excitedly announced that President Reagan would be coming to Nashville and speaking in the House of Representatives chamber. There was just one problem—the only person who could authorize the use of the House chamber was the House Speaker, and they had not talked with Speaker Ned McWherter.

When Governor Alexander's staff realized they had gotten the presidential cart ahead of the Speaker's horse, the group started trying to figure out how to gain Speaker McWherter's approval. They decided that President Reagan himself needed to ask Speaker McWherter to use the chamber for the appearance that Governor Alexander's team already had announced.

One of President Reagan's White House staff called for Speaker

Governor Ned McWherter wears some special boots and enjoys a laugh, perhaps at a joke about those same boots. Metropolitan Nashville Government Archives, *Nashville Banner* Collection.

McWherter and found him home in Dresden. She asked whether he could talk with the president about two o'clock that afternoon. Speaker McWherter responded: "I'd be happy to talk with the president, but I'll be fencing at that time."

Undeterred, the Reagan staffer asked: "Is there a phone at the club where you can be reached?"

McWherter paused, then replied: "Honey, my cows don't have any phones."

MCWHERTER'S SMOOTH AS BUTTER

As Speaker McWherter was running for governor, one long-time friend said admiringly: "That Ned is one smooth politician. I mean, he knows how to butter the bread on both sides and never let it drip off either one. . . . He can sic a dog on a cat and make the cat think he's his friend."[5]

GOVERNOR MCWHERTER'S SUGGESTIONS

As governor, Ned McWherter led for eight years using these principles: "Don't spend money you don't have" and "It's never too late to do what's right." One cabinet member allegedly once asked McWherter, "Governor, how do I know what is right?"

McWherter said, "Son, from time to time I'll be giving you some suggestions."

GOVERNOR MCWHERTER
AND THE FRESHMAN LEGISLATOR

We think that, years before, Governor McWherter had heard the following story of another governor, but near the end of his second term, he started telling the following story about himself and a freshman legislator. The legislator may actually have been one of our colleagues, though near the end of his administration McWherter sometimes put one of us in the story. The story Governor McWherter told went like this:

In my first term I needed to pass a three-cent gas tax increase to fund the road program. It was an increase that Governor Alexander and I knew would be needed to fully fund the program since back when we worked on the program when I was Speaker. But the votes for a gas tax increase were not easy to come by. So, I had a certain freshman legislator come to my office and explained the program to him and pointed out that some of these roads would be in his district. And I told him how I needed his help to fund the program.

He told me he just could not vote for any such tax increase.

Well, I kept trying to get the votes, and I still needed his vote. So I had him back in the office a second time, but he still said he could not help me.

But the vote was still close, and I still needed his vote. I couldn't get all the votes I needed, so I had him back a third time, this time to really explain the program to him.

When he sat down in front of my desk, I reached in the big drawer in my desk. I pulled out and put on top of my desk a child's toy yellow road grader. I asked that freshman legislator if he knew what it was. He told me that he did. I asked him what it was. He told me it was a road grader.

I held it up and turned it at various angles and told him: "You take a good look at it, Representative. Because if you don't vote for this gas tax bill, it will be the last road grader you see near your district while I am governor!"

MCWHERTER'S TOUGH GAME

When Michael Dukakis was running for president in the fall of 1988, controversy erupted over his membership in the American Civil Liberties Union, commonly referred to by its initials, ACLU. Governor McWherter was at a national governors' conference when a national television network reporter approached him about the controversy. The young woman from ABC stuck a microphone in McWherter's face with the camera rolling and asked: "Governor, are you concerned about the ACLU?"

McWherter paused, thought, and replied: "Yeah, I am. We play 'em in about two weeks and I don't think we match up very well."

Then he moved on, leaving the befuddled reporter with no comment that she could use.

Some say that if Governor Dukakis had been as nimble as Governor McWherter was, he would have been elected president.[6]

GOVERNOR MCWHERTER'S WARMTH IN WINTER

Marcia Jarvis, a secretary in the Conservation Committee of the House, took a group of citizens from Representative I. V. Hillis's district to visit with Governor McWherter. During the meeting a mayor told the governor that she had something she needed to tell him later.

After the meeting, the citizens left and Marcia began looking for the mayor but could not find her. As Marcia walked back into the governor's office, she heard the mayor tell Governor McWherter: "You're just the kind of man I need. Keep me warm in the winter and shady in the summertime!"

The governor just laughed.

MCWHERTER'S SYMPATHY

On a cold February morning in 1994, I (Cotton Ivy) was to speak at the annual Future Farmers of America breakfast in a Nashville hotel. As I neared the hotel on Capitol Hill, I proceeded through a traffic light that was green. All of a sudden a woman driving what looked like an army tank disguised as a 1980 Pontiac hit me. My car was knocked off the road and into the railing around the state's War Memorial Building.

I was transported to Vanderbilt's Trauma Unit by ambulance. My lips were split, four teeth were gone, my ribs were bruised, and I had a big knot on my head. I had not been in my room long before my friend and boss called. Governor McWherter told me: "Cotton, I went ahead and spoke at your meeting this morning. Don't worry about that. There is some state property damaged and you've totaled your state car. By the way, I've also talked to your doctor and he says you've lost a few teeth, but it's nothing to worry about."

I could not talk because my mouth had been sutured and my face was heavily bandaged, but I wrote on a pad a note and the nurse read it to the Governor. I wrote: "Tell him I wouldn't worry either if it was his or the doctor's teeth!"

GOVERNOR MCWHERTER'S CROWD

Governor McWherter told the following story repeatedly while he was governor and afterwards.

> It was late in the campaign against my friend Winfield Dunn. I was home in Weakley County, out on my farm. I needed some chewing tobacco, and so I went to the store in Palmersville. As I got out of my truck, there was an older gentleman sitting on the bench in front of the store.
>
> "Ned Ray, is that you?" the old-timer asked.
>
> "Yessir. Yessir, it is."
>
> "Ned Ray, I've been reading about you a lot in the newspapers."
>
> I'd been running for governor for two years, and we were in the heat of the last weeks of the election, and there was a story or two every day, and he sure should have been reading about me. I just told him: "Yessir. Yessir."
>
> "And I've been seeing you a lot on television."
>
> I had just spent three million dollars on television and I sure as —— hoped he had been seeing me on television. But I just said, "Yessir. Yessir."
>
> "But Ned Ray, let me tell you one thing. No matter how much fame or fortune you acquire, young man, the crowd at your funeral will still depend a —— lot on the weather!"

THE DIFFERENCE BETWEEN
BEING GOVERNOR AND CHAIRMAN

When I (Cotton Ivy) was the Commissioner of Agriculture, agricultural pavilions were being built around the state. Several that were influential in state government had an ag pavilion in their district. There were pavilions at Roane State Community College and Tennessee Tech. Of course, there was one at the University of Tennessee at Martin that Governor McWherter helped obtain when he was Speaker.

Governor McWherter and I, along with others, were touring the ag pavilions in July. We toured the ag pavilion on the Middle Tennessee State University campus in Murfreesboro, the hometown of Representative John Bragg. Outside it was about 98 degrees in the shade. We had our suit coats on our arms, our sleeves rolled up, and our ties loosened. As we walked into the pavilion, a cool breeze hit us in the face. I welcomed the air-conditioning and started putting my coat on. I looked around and Governor McWherter was standing there, astonished. He was in the only ag pavilion in the state that was air-conditioned. The pavilion in Martin had not been air-conditioned.

Finally, he said, "This thing is air-conditioned!"

I said, "Yes, sir, Governor, I think it is. I would imagine that it's the difference between being the governor of Tennessee and chairman of the Finance Ways and Means committee as Chairman Bragg is."

MCWHERTER DRIVING AGAIN

Ned McWherter served as Speaker of the Tennessee House of Representatives longer than anyone ever has: fourteen years. With the leadership position goes a driver and a car. Then he was twice elected governor, for eight more years, again with all the driving taken care of. So for almost a quarter century, he was being driven and not driving.

As Governor McWherter was giving his farewell speeches a few months before his term ended, he would say, "I'm looking forward to getting in my car and heading west on I-40 out of Nashville."

One day at a luncheon I (Cotton Ivy) was introducing McWherter and asked the crowd: "How would you like to be coming East on I-40 and meet a man that hadn't driven a car in thirty years?

"Turn signals hadn't been invented then.

"Reminds me of Aunt Mary being almost blind coming out of church Sunday and shaking hands with the preacher. She said, 'I couldn't hardly see you, preacher. Can't hardly tell daylight from dark. But thank the Lord I can still drive my car!'"

Judicial Branch:
Courts and Retorts

Some maintain that the judicial system has produced even more humorous stories than the executive and legislative branches of government. Some say lawyers have an unfair advantage because they are professional storytellers (a.k.a. liars).

In any event, there has been no shortage of humor in our courts and with the lawyers and judges who work in them. Following are excerpts from some humorous but actual opinions written by justices of the Tennessee Supreme Court and true stories involving Tennessee trial courts.

JUSTICE JOE HENRY

When Justice Joe Henry died, Justice William H. D. Fones wrote an essay entitled "In Honor of Joseph W. Henry: the Best of Joe."[1]

Justice Fones recalled Joe Henry as a soldier, trial attorney, legislator, politician, gubernatorial advisor and speechwriter. He noted that while Justice Henry excelled in all these roles, "He made his best marks as a Supreme Court Justice."[2]

Justice Henry himself, however, apparently thought his "best marks" were the humorous but unpublished parts of his opinions that his colleagues persuaded him to delete. He called those passages "The Best of Joe."[3]

For example, consider Justice Henry's original but unpublished opinion in the case affirming a woman's right to keep her maiden name. The original opinion began: "Rose Palermo, a Nashville lawyer, is by birth and by choice, Rosary Theresa Palermo.

"The theory of her lawsuit is that a rose by any other name is not as sweet."[4]

Then an adjutant general and later a Tennessee chief justice, Joe Henry smiles for the camera as paratroopers perform in this photo from the 1950s. Metropolitan Nashville Government Archives, *Nashville Banner* Collection.

THE CLASSIC CAT II

Justice Henry published one much enjoyed opinion involving the revocation of a beer permit for a notorious Nashville establishment, called the Classic Cat II, which was best known for its scantily clad women. A key issue was whether that establishment had allowed drunken persons to loiter.

Since the testimony of two soldiers, one the alleged "loitering drunk," was important, Justice Henry described their drinking this way. At mid-afternoon the two soldiers went to the establishment and imbibed "ten to fifteen" seven and sevens,[5] then left and settled down to some serious drinking, straight from a bottle of Seagram's V.O. That evening, they returned to the Classic Cat II and for two or three hours drank more seven and sevens. After reciting this, Justice Henry wrote of the alleged leading drinker:

> When we analyze this soldier's actions in terms of his stated intentions "to get bombed," the conclusion is inevitable that success crowned his efforts. While he lolled, loafed, and loitered about the Classic Cat satisfying his lickerish craving for liquor by lapping up

lavish libations, he fell from his chair, clutching his drink in his hand, into the waiting hands of vice squad officer McElhaney, who helped him up and took him to jail.

We subject his conduct to the most liberal standard that has come to the attention of the author of this opinion.

Not drunk is he who from the floor
Can rise alone and still drink more;
But drunk is he, who prostrate lies,
Without the power to drink or rise.[6]

This soldier fails the test. He was drunk—openly, visibly, notoriously, gloriously and uproariously drunk.

The Classic Cat II violated one of the great commandments by which "beer joints" must live. In summary and in short, in paraphrase and in idiom, the law "don't allow no [drunken] hanging around" beer establishments.

JUSTICE HENRY'S CIRCUS CANNONBALLER

Justice Joe Henry's humor was not limited to times when he was on the bench. For example, when the Tennessee Supreme Court selected Brooks McLemore as its executive secretary, Justice Henry told the story of "the time Cannonball Jones quit the old Cole Brothers Circus."

Justice Henry described Cannonball as the person "who was shot out of a cannon, hurtled through the air in a giant arc, and landed in a net on the other side of the tent." When Cannonball announced he was quitting, the owner of the circus protested that Cannonball could not quit because there was a contract. Furthermore, the owner protested Cannonball was the "star."

Cannonball still insisted on quitting, arguing that the circus owner could find someone to take his place.

"Perhaps so," said the owner, "but not a man of your *caliber.*"

JUSTICE JOHN WILKES

A century ago, another Giles countian named John S. Wilkes seemed to set the pattern Justice Henry followed decades later. The parallels between the two are striking.

Both lived in Pulaski.

Both fought in the major wars of their times—Commissary Captain Wilkes in the Civil War and Major Henry in World War II.

Both were key aides to governors. Wilkes was secretary to Governor Jonathan C. Brown in 1871–75. Henry was an advisor and speechwriter for Governors Frank Clement and Buford Ellington in the 1950s and 1960s.

They both led the Tennessee military. Wilkes was adjutant general while secretary to Governor Brown. Henry was adjutant general for six years as commanding general of the Tennessee National Guard.[7]

Both were Methodists. Both supported that church's Martin College in Pulaski.

Both loved humor. But while Justice Henry characterized his humorous passages deleted from his opinions as "The Best of Joe," Justice Wilkes either had no such editors or he overruled them. "The Best of John" may be found in his opinions published in the 1890s.

Justice Wilkes's opinions comprise perhaps the finest humor in Tennessee's published jurisprudence.[8] He was adept in using humor to illustrate an argument, deflate a critic, or describe the inadequacies of human beings faced with the inexplicable actions of animals. But Justice Wilkes's opinions best make his points for him. On the following pages are summaries of and quotations from actual opinions.

THE SUICIDAL PONY

Justice Wilkes described the case of *Lyons v. Stills* as "the case of a Texas pony that committed suicide."[9]

A Tennessee farmer who purchased a Texas pony was sued for refusing to pay for the pony. The purchaser had attempted to gentle, or calm down, the pony by hitching her to a post and leaving her for the night. Unfortunately, as Justice Wilkes wrote: "The next morning the defendant came around to see if the pony was making any progress towards gentle, and found her very quiet; in fact she was dead."

The purchaser testified he did not know what had caused the pony's death but thought it was because "she could not breathe." It seems the "slip halter" had slipped down and become tightened around the pony's nostrils.

The circuit court judge ruled for the Tennessee defendant, and

Justice Wilkes and the Tennessee Supreme Court agreed. Justice Wilkes wrote that the defendant had stated that "when he saw that pony had committed suicide he did not keep her any longer, and he therefore exercised his option to rescind the trade."

THE MARE AND THE TRAIN

The case of *Southern Railway Company v. Phillips* came out of James County.[10] A man named Phillips sued the railroad because his mare was injured on the railroad track when a freight train approached.

"The whistle was sounded, the bell was rung, and the brakes were applied." But instead of simply stepping off the track, the mare walked right down it, eventually coming to a bridge crossing a creek.

The train followed, stopping 120 yards from the mare and awaited the "pleasure and future movements of the mare." But the mare did not move. "It became necessary, therefore, to devise some means by which the train could run over the bridge without at the same time running over the mare."

Justice Wilkes reported that the train's fireman walked toward the mare to try to persuade her to leave the track, but instead "she ran over the bridge, stepping sometimes on the ties, and sometimes on the vacant spaces between them."

The mare was injured to the extent of thirty dollars.

Justice Wilkes wryly observed that while the case was presented through an agreed statement of facts, the briefs contained much that was not in the record.

He summarized the railroad attorney's arguments as contending that the mare "was guilty of the grossest contributory negligence in her efforts to cross the bridge, in stepping on the vacant spaces between the ties, and not on the ties themselves." Furthermore, counsel argued, "the fireman had a right to presume [the mare] would leave the track down the embankment, instead of attempting a trapeze performance in mid-air." Counsel for the plaintiff, however, argued otherwise. He did not insist that the fireman should have waded the creek to get around the mare, but instead "he should have gotten out to one side and 'shooed' her off the bank, like a woman shoos her chickens out of the flower bed."[11]

Justice Wilkes summarized plaintiff's counsel's most compelling argument this way, "that when the mare stopped at the trestle, and hesitated to cross it, she showed good horse sense, and, if the fireman had shown as much sense as the mare, the accident would not have happened."

Despite that reasoning, Justice Wilkes concluded that "inasmuch as the mare has recovered, the plaintiff ought not to recover . . ."

THOROUGHLY TRAINED COON DOGS

In the case of *Fink et al. v. Evans,* two McMinn County hounds disputed the right of way with another approaching train. Justice Wilkes summarized the consequences this way: "[O]ne was immediately transferred to the happy hunting grounds, where there are no railroads or other corporations, as they have no souls, and consequently no hereafter. The other was not killed, but was immediately converted into a thoroughly trained dog."

Justice Wilkes enjoyed sharing the testimony of litigants, particularly their descriptions. Consider this:

> Upon the question of the value of the dogs thus killed, plaintiff states that one was a red and white spotted hound, but without any spots. They were both good fox dogs, and also good 'possum and squirrel dogs, and were as good 'all round' dogs as he ever owned. . . . Other witnesses for plaintiff described the dogs as young, of common stock on the mother's side, but good parentage on the father's side, and they both resembled their father. They further state . . . "it was much easier to buy them than to sell them." . . . The witnesses for the [railroad company], however, state that [the dogs] had no real value, and that there is no market in McMinn County for hound dogs.

Justice Wilkes further analyzed the plaintiff's testimony that the dogs ran six hundred to seven hundred yards in the half-minute before they were struck. He opined that this would have been a pretty rapid pace, even for hound dogs worth as much as twenty-five dollars each, since the dogs would have been running faster than even the train.

The engineer testified that when he saw the dogs they were but thirty feet in front of him, so he blew the whistle. The plaintiff admitted the whistle was sounded, but insisted it was for the whole pack of dogs and not specifically for the ones that were run over.

Justice Wilkes considered that argument, but felt "it would require too great diligence for the engineer to whistle for each particular dog, more especially as he had no means of informing each dog that any special whistle was sounded for him."

The case finally turned on the dogs' being "guilty of the grossest contributory negligence, in running on the track, and in heeding neither whistle nor the approach of the engine. . . ."

KNOXVILLE'S DISORDERLY, INCARCERATED MULE

Perhaps Justice Wilkes's finest humor involved a mule incarcerated in Knoxville. To enjoy a classic, consider the following excerpts from *Mincey v. Bradburn:*

> This is a lawsuit arising out of the unlawful acts of a disorderly mule. He was found loitering about the streets of Knoxville, without any apparent business, no visible means of support, and no evidence of ownership, except a yoke on his neck. . . . Although he does not appear to have been drunk or boisterous, a vigilant officer of the peace of the city arrested him and took him to the lockup. . . .
>
> The pound keeper did not know whom he belonged to, and the mule made no disclosure of his ownership. The pound keeper, it appears[,] went to the market house, and inquired of the butchers if a mule had escaped from any one of them. Why he should suppose that a butcher's stall should be an appropriate place to find out the owner of a live mule does not appear. The pound keeper further inquired of such country people as he could find, if they knew of any one who had lost a mule. . . In the meantime the mule was kept in close confinement, and refused to be interviewed. . . . [T]he pound master advertised in the *Knoxville Journal & Tribune* that the mule would be sold. . . . Mr. Smith, the purchaser, sold the mule to Mincey, but for what sum does not appear. Mincey, it appears, bought the mule in good faith, and did not know that he had ever been arrested or confined in the city lockup, or that he had been sold by the city. So far as he knew, the mule had the usual good reputation of his species. In the meantime, Mr. Bradburn, to whom the mule belonged, missed him from his corn crib, and supposed he had gone to Sevier County, where he came from originally. . . .

Mr. Bradburn did not see the advertisement in the *Journal & Tribune.* Probably he did not take the paper, but read the *Sentinel.* Counsel says that the advertisement was put in an obscure place. Exactly what he means the court to infer from that we are unable to see. The court cannot judicially know there is anything obscure in any Knoxville paper, unless it is the reports of Supreme Court opinions, and these appear to be obscure only to the lawyers who lose their cases. After the sale, and plaintiff found out where his mule was, he replevied[12] him. The case was tried before the court and jury in the court below, and plaintiff was successful. . . . The city comes in, however, by counsel, and complains earnestly at the charge of the circuit judge . . . that the pound master should immediately, upon impounding the animal, make the advertisement, and that if the mule was impounded on the 7th, and not advertised till the 12th it was not a compliance with the ordinance. . . .

The city attorney insists that this is requiring too great a degree of diligence on the part of the pound master. . . .

The argument is that the word immediately, as used in the ordinance, does not mean instantaneously; that the pound keeper must have sufficient time to shut the pound gate so as to keep the mule in, before he starts to the printing office; that, after he does start, he may proceed in a brisk walk, and is not required to run; that after he gets there time must be allowed to set up the matter in type, and there must be a delay until the hour when the paper is printed and ready for distribution; and that the pound keeper is not required to get out an extra.

We are satisfied the learned judge did not mean to require such dispatch as this. . . .

Now, if the mule was the party complaining, the Court would feel disposed to say the delay was too great, as it does not appear that the mule had anything to eat during his stay as the city's guest. But neither the city nor the owner has any ground of complaint.

It is said by counsel that the other question presented is an exceedingly important one, and we approach it with a deep feeling of responsibility.

Counsel for plaintiff says that the ordinance is unreasonable, and the charge was necessary to correct a great and growing evil. What this evil is the record does not disclose. It is not alleged that any great trust or combine is being formed in impounded mules, and it is not shown that any trust at all exists as to mules running loose. . . .

The argument of the city attorney seems to be that, if a hog may be sold in three days, a mule might be sold in two days, since he is much more of a nuisance, and much more dangerous to keep, and the city ought not to be expected to remain forever on guard. Now, we do not desire to say anything disrespectful of or derogatory to the mule. He has no posterity to protect and keep alive his memory. The ordinance applies to all animals, and we are of the opinion that two days' advertisement is not enough. . . . We feel . . . the ordinance unreasonable, and the judgment must be affirmed.

JUDGE ANDREW JACKSON

Andrew Jackson resigned from the U.S. Senate in 1798 to serve Tennessee on the Supreme Court of Law and Equity. One day Jackson was holding court when a huge man named Russell Bean, who had been indicted for cutting off the ears of a child, "paraded before the court cursing judge, jury, and then marched out the door." Jackson ordered Bean arrested. The sheriff went to get the offender, but soon returned empty-handed with the excuse that apprehending Bean was impossible. Bean had threatened to shoot anyone who touched him. Jackson stood and announced that court was recessed for ten minutes.

As Bean stood in a crowd cursing and flaunting his weapons, Jackson walked straight toward Bean with pistols in both hands.

"Now," Judge Jackson roared, "surrender or I'll blow you through."

Bean looked into Jackson's blazing eyes, then surrendered.

When Bean later was asked why he gave up to Jackson after having defied the sheriff and a posse, Bean replied: "When he came up, I looked him in the eye and I saw 'shoot' and there hadn't been 'shoot' in the eye of anyone else, so I said 'Hoss, it's time to sing small.'"

EVANS SMITH'S SUITS

Evans Smith was a rather interesting and colorful native of Henry County, Tennessee. One of Evans Smith's talents was that he was an amazing witness—an almost omnipresent witness in southwest Henry County. Things would happen when no one knew that Evans Smith was around, but when the time for a trial came, it turned out that he had seen exactly what had happened.

Through Smith's public service as a witness, he became a friend of Aaron Brown, an exceptionally fine attorney in Paris. In the middle portion of the twentieth century, Aaron Brown also served in the Tennessee Senate, was a delegate to a Constitutional Convention, and was considered gubernatorial material. After decades as an attorney, he eventually became a fine judge, serving as a chancellor.

Attorney Aaron Brown was known to partake of some of the liquefied grain products. And he also smoked cigars. Sometimes the combination would result in Brown burning holes in his suits. And since Aaron Brown and Evans Smith were good friends and the same size, Mr. Brown would give Mr. Smith his cigar-burned suits.

One day a Henry countian named Billy Owens saw the Sunday-suited Evans Smith and commented, "Evans, you are dressed right good."

"Well, thank you Mr. Owens," Evans Smith replied.

"How can you afford such nice suits?"

"Mr. Brown gives 'em to me."

"Why does Mr. Brown give you suits?" asked Owens.

"Cause he's a friend of mine," replied Evans Smith.

"Well, I'm Mr. Brown's friend also, but he never gives me a suit."

To which came the quick reply: "What your trouble is, is you ain't never testified!"[13]

EVANS SMITH'S SHOATS

A Henry County man was run over by a train. Attorney Aaron Brown brought suit on behalf of the family of the deceased. Attorney Brown sued the L & N Railroad for a million dollars. A year and a half later the trial was about to begin in federal court in Jackson. Suddenly, two weeks before trial, Evans Smith said he had seen the train wreck.

At the trial Evans Smith was questioned by the defense counsel about what he was doing at the time the train ran over the deceased.

"I was feeding my shoats."

"Will you explain," the lawyer asked for the benefit of the jurors there in the more urban city of Jackson, "what a shoat is?"

Evans Smith looked hard at the lawyer, amazed at the question. Finally, knowing the lawyer must be smarter than he sounded, he replied: "Awww, Mr. Moss," Evans Smith replied, "you know what a shoat is!"[14]

AARON BROWN AND "CUTWORM" PIERCE

Aaron Brown was awfully good friends with and a running buddy of "Cutworm" Pierce, who had served as Henry County circuit court clerk. When Aaron Brown became chancellor, he appointed Cutworm his clerk and master.

One of Cutworm's unofficial responsibilities as clerk and master was to drive Chancellor Brown when the chancellor would consume liquefied grain products.

One day after court adjourned, the chancellor imbibed some liquefied grain. Not content to drink alone, he pushed Cutworm, who abstained from alcohol, to have a drink with him.

Failing to persuade Cutworm to break his abstinence from whiskey, the chancellor tried to get him to drink some vodka. The chancellor assured Cutworm that no one could know because no one would smell the vodka.

Cutworm considered that briefly, then replied: "No sir, you keep it yourself. I'd want somebody to smell it and to know I'd been drinking if I was going to act as big a fool as you!"

I CAN'T HEAR

District Attorney Tommy Thomas tells of prosecuting a case in Juvenile Court in which a Japanese student was the victim. An area attorney was defending a local juvenile.

The victim spoke no English, so the court had to find a translator, and the translator was there and ready. When prosecutor Thomas asked the questions, the translator translated the question into Japanese. The young victim replied quietly. Suddenly the defense attorney stood and objected: "Your Honor, I can't hear the witness!"

General Thomas replied: "It doesn't matter. She's speaking Japanese."

The defense attorney pondered that for a moment, then quietly said: "Oh. That's right. I forgot."

EAST TENNESSEE JUSTICE

An East Tennessee general sessions judge had a heavy docket one Monday morning. All the law enforcement officers were at the courthouse to help prosecute the cases. One highway patrolman had the radar goods on a local citizen doing seventy-one miles an hour in a fifty-five-mile-per-hour zone. The judge heard the rather convincing evidence, but then dismissed the case.

The patrolman was upset and waited around for hours to talk to the judge in his chambers. The trooper demanded, "Judge, please explain to me why you ignored my proof on Mr. Jones."

The judge looked the patrolman in the eye and said, "Let me ask you this question. Have you ever given a fellow trooper a ticket?"

"Of course not."

"Have you ever given a sheriff or a deputy a ticket?"

"No," was the reluctant reply.

"Have you ever given a policeman a ticket?"

"Not that I remember."

"Well," the judge concluded, "you take care of your folks and I'll take care of mine."

JUSTICE, TIRES, WE DO IT ALL

Obion County General Sessions Judge Eb Maness kept a telephone right on the bench in the courtroom. One day attorney David Hayes was in the middle of an impassioned closing argument when the phone rang. The judge immediately picked up the phone and said: "Judge Maness here."

The judge listened a moment, then asked the caller: "Yeah, hey, can you get those tires done by noon?"

There was another pause while the judge listened to the service station attendant. David Hayes stood in shocked silence, not quite believing what was going on.

"Great, great!" the judge exclaimed.

He hung the phone up and told the completely distracted attorney: "Move along, counselor, move along."

MAGAZINE LAW

Attorney David Hayes had been appointed to represent an indigent criminal defendant in Obion County General Sessions Court. Attorney

Hayes made what he thought was a well-founded motion, but Judge Eb Maness ruled against him.

After the case was over, the young attorney went to see the judge outside the courtroom.

When Hayes showed the judge the page from the pocket part of the *Tennessee Code Annotated* with the provision of law clearly on point, the judge thought a moment and replied: "Now, David, I'm just not going to hold to any of that *magazine law*!"

NOT SETTLING FOR APPLES

A woman struck in the head by a bag of apples tossed by a grocery store's irate customer sued the store for one million dollars.

Mary Lou Settle alleged in her lawsuit that Boyd L. Davis of Hendersonville was complaining to a clerk at a Kroger grocery store that he had been overcharged for a five-pound bag of apples when he threw the produce at the clerk. The flying bag of apples missed its mark and struck Ms. Settle in the head, according to the suit.

Mr. Davis was arrested for assault and battery and breach of peace and spent two days in the Sumner County Jail. According to police reports, Ms. Settle was taken to Hendersonville Hospital and treated for minor injuries.

Ms. Settle claimed in the lawsuit, filed in Sumner County Circuit Court, that she still suffered from chronic pain and would require further medical care as a result of the incident.

"The blow to her head was so severe that her brain swelled such that she suffered seizures and convulsions, blurred vision, nausea, dizziness, extreme and severe pressure within the head, losing sleep and remaining in chronic pain since the incident," the lawsuit alleged.

Mr. Davis told police he remembered complaining about the price of the apples and "also that he intended to throw the apples, but could not remember anything else past that point."

JUDGE WEINMAN FOR THE DEFENSE

Memphis attorney Bill Haltom tells of a memorable time when he was in Shelby County Criminal Court for arraignments. Several defendants and their attorneys were lined up. Judge Bernie Weinman asked one lonely defendant if he had an attorney. The man said he had talked with one. Judge Weinman asked with whom he had talked.

The nervous defendant, recalling the last name he'd heard when the bailiff intoned, "Judge Bernie Weinman presiding," replied, "Bernie Weinman."

There was great laughter.

The judge asked the now bewildered defendant, "What did this Weinman fellow say?"

"He said that if I paid him a thousand dollars, he could take care of everything."

WHO GETS THE MULE?

The fact that our imperfect jury system usually works is perhaps best illustrated by the story of the Tennessee jury that was empanelled in the criminal trial of a man charged with stealing a mule.

As the proof developed in the trial, the evidence was rather overwhelming that the man in fact did steal the mule. But the proof also showed that the defendant was basically an honorable and decent fellow who was really down on his luck and desperately needed the mule to help him on his family farm.

After deliberating, the jury returned and the foreman announced the verdict: "Not guilty, but he has to give back the mule."

The wise and learned judge said, "Ladies and gentlemen of the jury, I must reject your verdict. It is an inconsistent verdict, and I must request that you resume your deliberations and return a consistent verdict."

The jurors looked at one another and then filed back into the jury room.

Five minutes later they returned.

"Have you reached another verdict?" inquired the judge.
"Yes, we have, Your Honor," reported the foreman. "Not guilty and he can keep that mule!"

National Government:
Tennesseans with Potomac Fever

Tennessee has produced many outstanding leaders. In the first seven decades after it became a state in 1796, the state gave the country three presidents: Andrew Jackson, James K. Polk, and Andrew Johnson. In 1956 alone, three Tennesseans were touted for the national ticket: Governor Frank Clement, Senator Albert Gore Sr., and Senator Estes Kefauver. As the twentieth century came to a close, again three Tennesseans were seriously discussed as presidential timber: former Governor Lamar Alexander, Senator Fred Thompson, and Vice President Al Gore Jr. As of this writing, Gore is the first Tennessean to become a major party's presidential nominee since James K. Polk 156 years earlier.

Less well known and perhaps less historic are the contributions Tennesseans serving in Washington make to the wealth of humor we can enjoy. Consider the following stories of Tennesseans serving in our national government.

SENATOR BAKER'S LANDING

It was a tough night for flying, or at least for landing. Senator Howard Baker, his press secretary Ron McMahan, and some members of the media were flying in a small plane into a small Tennessee airport. The clouds were low and the visibility not much when the pilot attempted the landing.

At the last moment, the pilot aborted the landing, pulled the plane's nose back up, and went around again. His voice came over the intercom, explaining that he thought it was best that they take another attempt at landing.

That got everyone's attention. They peered out into the clouds in the darkness, seeing nothing resembling the earth.

The pilot brought the plane back around, and they could feel the plane slowing and descending again. But once again the pilot yanked the controls back, pushed the throttle forward, and pulled the plane out of its descent into who knew what.

The pilot came on the intercom again, apologizing and saying that they would have to take another try. Baker's press secretary spoke for everyone when he yelled to the pilot: "Land this ———— thing! There's not enough Jack Daniel's to miss it again!"

SENATOR MCKELLAR
AND THE FOUNDING OF OAK RIDGE

Kenneth McKellar served Tennessee and the nation as a U.S. Senator from 1917 until 1953. He was the only Tennessean ever elected to six terms in the U.S. Senate. For many years, he chaired the Senate

U.S. Senator Kenneth McKellar of Memphis does not look like all of his duties were weighing too heavily upon him in this 1935 photo. Metropolitan Nashville Government Archives, *Nashville Banner* Collection.

Appropriations Committee and wielded enormous influence and sometimes outright control of national funding.

During World War II, Secretary of War Henry Stimson hinted in a meeting that he needed McKellar to hide two billion dollars in an appropriations bill for a secret project that might bring an end to the war. That night, McKellar could not sleep. He returned to Stimson's office the next day to inquire further.

Eventually President Franklin D. Roosevelt himself summoned McKellar to the White House to repeat the request. President Roosevelt asked, "Senator McKellar, can you hide two billion dollars for this supersecret national defense project?"

Senator McKellar immediately replied, "Well, Mr. President, of course I can. And where in Tennessee do you want me to hide it?"

That is how Oak Ridge came to be.

NATIONAL CANDIDATES

In 1956, Tennessee had not just one or even two but no less than three potential nominees for the Democratic national ticket. Senators Kefauver and Gore and Governor Clement all thought they

Three figures prominent not only in Tennessee but also nationally were U.S. Senators Albert Gore Sr. (left) and Estes Kefauver (center) and Governor Frank Clement (right). Metropolitan Nashville Government Archives, *Nashville Banner* Collection.

might be looking at a president or at least a vice president in the mirror when they shaved in the morning.

The Democratic National Convention was most entertaining to Tennesseans that year. Senator Kefauver eventually was the vice presidential nominee. Before that occurred, however, Governor Clement delivered the keynote address, and there was significant support for putting him on the ticket. Furthermore, after Adlai Stevenson of Illinois was selected as the presidential nominee, Alabama, first in the roll call for nominations, yielded to Tennessee so Jarred Maddux could offer Albert Gore Sr. in nomination for the vice presidency.

Senator Gore's wife, Pauline, later said she had been picking vice-presidential lice off her husband for a year but evidently had missed one.

SENATOR KEFAUVER AND "HOW'S YOUR DAD?"

Senator Estes Kefauver was good about remembering faces and names. But even he at times grew tired. At one gathering, as he shook hands in a large crowd, he saw the son of an old acquaintance.

"How's your dad?" Kefauver asked.

"He's dead," the young man responded sadly.

In July 1952, Senator Estes Kefauver and his wife, Nancy, push their baggage to a plane at Washington National Airport on their way to the Democratic National Convention in Chicago. He carries his trademark coonskin cap, while Nancy carries what was described as a "pure white coonskin cap." Metropolitan Nashville Government Archives, *Nashville Banner* Collection.

Kefauver tenderly expressed his regrets, and then he went back to shaking hands in the crowd. After a while, Kefauver again encountered the somewhat familiar face of the son of his friend.

"How's your dad?" the weary Kefauver cheerfully asked the young man.

"He's still dead."

AL GORE SR. AND THE HONORABLE GENTLEMEN

Albert Gore Sr. left the United States House of Representatives and entered the U.S. Senate. In one of his first exchanges on the floor of the Senate, he used a circumlocution common in the House of Representatives and referred to a senator as "the Honorable Gentleman."

Unfortunately, however, the Senate uses different terms, including specifically "the Distinguished Senator." The senator whom Gore referred to took great offense. He chastised Gore for his improper appellation for a senator.

Gore apologized profusely, assuring the senator: "I shall never again make the mistake of calling you 'Honorable.'"

SENATOR AL GORE SR. AND THE BOYS

When the United States Supreme Court decided in *Brown v. Board of Education* that "separate but equal" schools were *not* equal, the South was inflamed. Southern politicians drafted the "Southern Manifesto," declaring their opposition to and defiance of the Supreme Court.

Only three southern senators refused to sign the manifesto, and two of those were Tennessee's senators, Estes Kefauver and Albert Gore Sr.[1] Not long afterwards, one night Senator Gore's sleep was interrupted by a telephone call.

"Senator, me and the boys are shooting a little pool and talking about things and about you and Senator Kefauver, and we just wanted you to know what we thought."

"Well, Billy," Senator Gore responded, recognizing the otherwise unidentified and intoxicated voice, "I always want to know the views of my constituents." He paused, then added, "Even at two o'clock in the morning."

Senator Albert Gore Sr. and his wife, Pauline LaFon Gore, play with their
daughter, Nancy, in a Tennessee state park. At the time this photo was
taken, their second child, Albert Gore Jr., was not yet born. Tennessee
State Library and Archives.

"Senator, it's about this here race thing. We want you to know
how we feel about these colored folks.

"We don't want to eat with 'em.

"We don't want to sleep with 'em.

"We don't want to go to school with 'em.

"We don't want to go to church with 'em."

Senator Gore interrupted with a single, incisive question: "Billy,
do you want to go to heaven with them?"

There was a long silence on the other end.

"No, Senator, we don't. I guess we just want . . . *to go to* ———
with you and Kefauver!"

ALBERT GORE'S STRAWBERRIES

Mayor Al Bissell told this story on his good friend, U.S. Senator Al
Gore Sr.

Well, I was in Washington one time and I went over to see Albert
in his Senate office. I remember it just like it was yesterday.

Pauline [Mrs. Albert Gore Sr.] came running out and grabbed me
by my coat sleeve and said, "Al, Albert's in a frightful mood today.
See if you can't humor him a little."

I said, "What's the matter, Pauline?"

"Oh, there were a bunch of people in here from Humboldt [the Strawberry Capital of West Tennessee] and they just jumped all over Albert because he didn't know the price of strawberries. See if you can't humor him a little. He's just upset."

So, I went into Albert's office and I could see right off that he was in a sour mood. I asked him what was the matter.

[Here Al Bissell would screw his mouth into a funnel shape and imitate Al Gore Sr.]

"Al, these folks from Humboldt were in here this morning. They are having some sort of problem with the strawberry market, and they want me to do something about it. Do you know that they actually got upset with me because I didn't know the price of strawberries? Can you imagine?"

And Ole Albert's face would get redder than a beet, and he'd squirm around in his chair.

"Why, Al," he'd say, "I'm a United States Senatooor.[2] I've got world problems to deal with. I've got to be concerned with Red Chiner and things like that. A United States Senatooor can't be expected to know the price of strawberries.

"Al, what do you recommend I do?"

I took a deep breath and asked him, "Albert, how many votes do you reckon you'll get in Red Chiner in the next election?"

"Why none. What's that got to do with it?"

So, I took another deep breath because I knew he wouldn't like it and I said: "Then, Senator, I recommend you learn the price of strawberries."

SENATOR HOWARD BAKER JR.
AND MAYOR AL BISSELL

Oak Ridge Mayor Al Bissell, a big Democrat, often told his good Republican friend Howard Baker Jr., the majority leader of the U.S. Senate: "Howard, you're a nice man. You know, Howard, you're almost nice enough to be a Democrat. Howard, I'm gonna see if I can't get you named a Democrat."

The legendary Congressman Jimmy Quillen (left) and former Governor
Winfield Dunn joined together in January 1986 as Dunn runs for governor again. The two clashed back in 1974 when Dunn vetoed a bill to
create a medical school in Quillen's northeast Tennessee district. Metropolitan Nashville Government Archives, *Nashville Banner* Collection.

CONGRESSMAN QUILLEN'S
POKER-PLAYING SHERIFF

Congressman Jimmy Quillen used to tell the story of the East Tennessee sheriff that loved to play poker. His wife and staff knew this
was top priority—so they kept close tabs on him after five o'clock.
Then the sheriff came up with the idea of gathering four or five of
his friends in a secluded, wooded area after lunch, so they would have
all afternoon for the game.

The sheriff would bring a jug of confiscated moonshine, some
chasers, and a quilt to deal the cards on. All the other players would
come in one car and park by the sheriff's car. The sheriff would leave
his motor running.

One day they asked why he never shut off his car engine. The sheriff explained: "If the Highway Patrol ever comes, I want my motor
hot and all of y'all are under arrest. Now deal the cards."

CONGRESSMAN JONES, SENATOR SASSER, AND SPEAKER O'NEILL

In the 1980s, I (Cotton Ivy) was called on several times to come to Washington to serve as a master of ceremonies or to give a Tennessee welcome to folks. One such occasion was a fundraiser for Congressman Ed Jones. The congressman's wife, "Miss Lou," was an expert at Tennessee country ham breakfasts and Congressman Jones used her talent to solicit funds. Congressman Jones had flown me all the way to Washington to do twelve minutes of humor.

This particular morning was a special occasion attended by the Speaker of the House, Tip O'Neill, and other dignitaries I had seen on television but never met. I was seated next to Speaker O'Neill. The Speaker obviously knew how to eat, but that morning I showed him how to eat red-eye gravy, ham meat, and sorghum on a biscuit. He got the hang of it quickly, downing eight or ten of those ham and biscuits.

Senator Jim Sasser was the master of ceremonies. With all the dignitaries there, Senator Sasser started my introduction. I did not know Senator Sasser personally, but of course he was kinfolk to everybody, claiming to have been born in almost every county in Tennessee and planning to be buried in most of them. While introducing me Sasser kept saying that he knew me better than he really knew me, talking about what a wonderful humorist I was, a man that Sasser said he had known intimately through the years, that our families were close. As Sasser went on and on, using up my twelve minutes, I realized the Senator had forgotten my name. Struggling to recall it, Sasser kept talking about how close we were. Finally, after we were so close that we had to be at least double first cousins if not brothers, he admitted his dilemma. He looked out at the audience and confessed: "I have had a mental block. I have forgotten the speaker's name."

Speaker Tip O'Neill, who called me the "funny man" and never knew my name either, looked over at my name tag, read it backwards, and loudly announced: "Senator, his ———— name is Ivy Cotton!"

LIKE MISTER ED

When John Tanner was running for Congressman Ed Jones's seat after Mr. Ed had announced his retirement, a group of people in Stewart

County had an event for Tanner at a restaurant. There was a good crowd, and it was a good event.

As the event was ending, Congressman Tanner shook hands with everybody out front and wanted to shake hands with the people back in the kitchen. He asked the proprietor whether that would be all right, and he allowed that it would be. When Tanner came back out of the kitchen, the owner asked him: "Are you going to be like Ed Jones?"

Tanner replied, "Well, I would like to be. Of course, Mr. Ed has endorsed me. He's been helping me. And I've learned a lot from him through the years. I don't know that I can be as good a congressman as Mr. Ed is, but I'd like to think I could learn from him and try hard to be. That's what I'd like to do—be like him."

The proprietor immediately started in: "That ———— scoundrel has been a sorry ————! He has never cared for anybody but the farmers. He's never done anything for us around here. He's a no count excuse for a congressman!"

John Tanner looked down at his feet. Then he looked around the restaurant. Finally, he looked back at the proprietor and said: "Well, I didn't say I was going to be *exactly* like him. . . ."

HADN'T PLANNED ON GOING THAT HIGH

Congressman John Tanner held a listening meeting in the unincorporated community of Dancyville in Haywood County. A gentleman named King thanked Congressman Tanner for coming to see them, noting that they didn't get many Members of Congress in a small place like Dancyville. Congressman Tanner, touched by the gentleman's appreciation and respect, told Mr. King that if ever he could be of help to Mr. King, then to please let him know.

The next Saturday the congressman was home watching a football game on the television when the phone rang. It was Mr. King.

"Congressman, you said if ever you could help me, you would."

"Yessir, Mr. King, I sure did. What can I do to help you?"

"Well, it's about this road down here. It sure needs some work."

Congressman Tanner thought a moment, recalling that there was no federal highway at Dancyville.

"Mr. King, is it a state or a county road?"

"County road, Congressman."

"Well, have you thought about calling your county executive, Mr. Franklin Smith? You know, he's over Haywood County matters."

"Yes sir, I know he's over all of Haywood County. But I hadn't wanted to call him. I hadn't planned on going that high."

THE JOHN TANNER STATUE

Congressman John Tanner's field representative, Joe Hill, and Union City funeral home director Barry White have been known to enjoy a prank. One day they worked up a story about the fictitious statue of Congressman Tanner that the proud citizens of Obion County allegedly wanted to erect on the courthouse lawn. Barry White called Washington and asked to speak to Congressman Tanner about an urgent matter. As soon as White got Tanner on the line, he explained in enthusiastic detail how Obion County needed to have statues of both of its congressmen. They were going to put the one of Tanner near the existing statue of the late Congressman Fats Everett.

The Congressman couldn't believe it. But he did. He immediately called Joe Hill in Union City, as Hill knew he would. Tanner told Hill the statue story and raised thunder. Hill muzzled his laughter and let his boss spout. Tanner told Hill in no uncertain terms what a crazy idea it was. He concluded that Hill absolutely had to stop this ridiculous project before it got anywhere.

Hill let the silence build a moment, then firmly replied: "John, it's too late. Barry's already raised seven or eight thousand dollars!"

Now the silence was on Tanner's end. Finally, he moaned: "Awwwww, Jooooooe!"

SOUTHERN SPEAKERS

President Clinton attended Vice President Gore's Family Re-Union Conference in Nashville. After Secretary of Education Richard Riley spoke, President Clinton said: "As you can tell, he's from South Carolina, and the vice president and I like him because he makes it sound like we don't have an accent."

VICE PRESIDENT GORE'S WAITER

For some years Al Gore has told a story about a politician who came to town for a banquet. As the politician sat at the head table, a waiter came by and put a pat of butter on his plate.

The politician asked, "Can I have another pat of butter?"

The waiter replied, "Sorry. One pat per person."

"Well," the indignant politician said, "I guess you don't know who I am." And the politician began telling the waiter just how important he was.

When he finally was done, the waiter said, "I guess you don't know who I am."

"I guess I don't. Who are you?"

"I'm the guy," the waiter said, "who controls the butter."

GORE ON REPUBLICANS AND DEMOCRATS

Vice President Gore recalls the words of the late Senator S. I. Hayakawa from California who used to describe the two parties this way.

A Republican sees a drowning man fifty feet from shore, throws him a twenty foot rope, and tells him swimming the thirty feet is good for his character.

A Democrat throws the drowning man a one-hundred-foot rope, then walks away looking for other good deeds to do.

TIPPER GORE'S TITLES

The day before the Super Tuesday presidential primary elections in 1996, Tipper Gore came to Nashville. She related that people often weren't sure what to call her. She has been called a number of things, she said with a smile.

Tipper said she has been called "The Second First Lady," "Lady Gore," "The Vice President's Wife." But her favorite title was given by a very enthusiastic, if somewhat confused, minister who introduced her as "The Second Lady of the Vice!"

One-Liners:
Stick It to 'Em Quick

Some of the best political humor is not a long story, or even a short one. It is the one-liner, the quick remark that delights or deflates, pierces or puns. Following are some of our favorites, as well as a few humorous and quick hits that take an extra line or two.

POLITICS

Politics—a compound word from "poli," which means "many," and "tics," which means bloodsuckers.

WHY WASHINGTON TOLD THE TRUTH

Representative John Bragg told of a child who asked who George Washington was. An adult responded this way: "Well, he was the first U.S. president, of course. And the only one ever elected with no opposition! Which may explain why he never told a lie."

FUTURE CONGRESSMAN

"I've decided what I want to be when I grow up," a young Bob Clement announced.

"What's that?" asked his father, the governor.

"A prisoner," said Bob. "They have the most fun."

REGARDLESS

Governor Frank Clement once wrote, "If a man wants to buy an automobile, get married or run for political office, he will do just that regardless of advice."

CHOOSING WORDS

Senator Howard Baker once told his father-in-law, Senator Everett Dirksen of Illinois, "You don't choose your words for what they mean; you choose them for how they taste."

BAKER'S GIFT

Expressing his admiration for his friend, Lamar Alexander claimed: "Howard Baker . . . had a gift for being partisan and ambitious without seeming either."

U.S. Senator Howard Baker Jr. finds a pleasant place to sit on the steps of the U.S. Capitol with a group of 4-H students from Tennessee. Metropolitan Nashville Government Archives, *Nashville Banner* Collection.

U.S. Senators Bill Brock (left) and Howard Baker (center) share a laugh with a friend. The two represented Tennessee in the Senate together from 1971 to 1977. Metropolitan Nashville Government Archives, *Nashville Banner* Collection.

BAKER'S ADVICE

Early in his 1995–96 campaign for the presidency, former governor Lamar Alexander telephoned former senator Howard Baker. Alexander told Baker: "I've decided to walk across New Hampshire, from Concord to the sea."

Baker replied, "If I were doing it, I'd walk from Portsmouth to the sea."

"Portsmouth *is* on the sea," Alexander said, thinking Baker must be confused. But the sage Baker, anything but confused, said simply: "I know."

LOTS OF GOVERNORS BUT ONLY ONE DOLLY

At the opening of the Dollywood theme park in Sevier County in 1986, Governor Lamar Alexander rode through the crowd with Dolly Parton in an open car. Several people shouted, "Governor, would you please move over so we can see Dolly?"

Alexander said he learned this lesson: "If you want to be noticed, don't ride in a convertible with Dolly Parton."

MCWHERTER'S NOT OPPOSING

Governor Ned McWherter had this to say about bills designed to alter his TennCare health care reform: "I'm not opposed to them, I just don't want them to pass."[1]

TOUCHED

At a five-hundred-dollar-a-head fundraiser in Knoxville, Jim Sasser acknowledged: "I'm touched that you came out, but probably not touched as much as you were."

SASSER ON QUAYLE

Senator Jim Sasser said that Vice President Dan Quayle was asked how to spell Mississippi. According to Sasser, Quayle allegedly replied: "Do you mean the state or the river?"

GORE AND QUAYLE

A sign on the floor of 1992 Democratic National Convention read: "Al Gore has written more books than Dan Quayle has read."

GORE'S CODE NAME

Appearing at the annual Gridiron Club dinner in Washington, Al Gore admitted: "Al Gore is so boring his Secret Service code name is 'Al Gore.'"

THE SOURCE OF WISDOM

Vice President Gore told a story he said he heard in Tennessee about an old man renowned for his wisdom.

"Somebody once asked the wise old man how come he was so smart. 'Well . . . I've got good judgment,' he said. 'Good judgment comes from experience. And experience? Well . . . that comes from bad judgment.'"

Former Senator Albert Gore Sr. helps his son kick off his United States Senate campaign in Carthage in 1984, as Albert Gore Jr. holds his son, Albert III.

A SLOW-GROWING TREE

Vice President Gore quoted President Kennedy as telling a story about a French general who asked his gardener to plant a tree.

"Oh, this tree grows slowly," the gardener said. "It won't mature for a hundred years."

"Then there's no time to lose," the general said. "Plant it this afternoon."

ON DEMOCRATIC UNITY—
OR THE LACK THERE OF

Speaking in Chicago, Vice President Gore quoted an old Chicago newspaperman, Finley Peter Dunne of the *Daily News* as observing through his quintessential Irish saloon keeper Mr. Dooley, "Th' dimmycratic party ain't on speakin' terms with itself."

LOVE IN THE HOUSE

State Representative Harold Love of Nashville repeatedly campaigned for reelection using this slogan: "Keep Love in the House."

In 1998, Representative Love's son, Harold Love Jr., ran for his late father's seat with this slogan: "Put Love Back in the House."

24,000 BOOS

After he was grilled for two hours by the House Transportation Committee, Commissioner of Transportation and former Southeastern Conference basketball official Dale Kelley claimed, "The abuse doesn't mean a thing to me. I've been booed by 24,000 people at once."

THEY'RE HERE

Stewart County businessman Don Cherry warned Congressman John Tanner before he went into the courthouse for an open meeting, "There's five ———— fools in this county, and every one of 'em is upstairs!"

ON THE ELECTORATE

Representative Charles Curtiss, after serving a couple of terms, concluded: "No matter how hard you work, you will never make all [the citizens] glad, but if you are not real careful, you can sure make all of them mad!"

CINDERELLA

During a Family Re-Union Conference in Nashville, the community involvement coordinator for the Hamilton County schools told of taking Governor Don Sundquist to a play.

President Clinton responded, "I'm glad you took the governor to see Cinderella. I hope you got him home before midnight."

HANK VS. FATE, FIDELITY VS. FATBACK

When Hank Hillin announced his plan to run for sheriff against incumbent . . . Fate Thomas, he came up with four by-words that would dominate his regime: "Fidelity, honesty, integrity, and dignity." Which prompted one wag to give Sheriff Thomas his own four-word slogan: "Fatback, hominy, grits, and cornbread."

In the little volume called *You Are So Nashville If . . . By the Readers of the* Nashville Scene, a number of readers shared their own special insights into Tennessee politics, at least and especially in Nashville. Their one-liners follow. Each makes sense by prefacing it with these words: "You are so Nashville if . . ."[2]

You haven't realized that the collective IQ of our state and city political leadership is exceeded by that of a single lobotomized angleworm.

Dale Robertson

Your vote can be swayed by free BBQ.

Jim Steel

You run for city government because you have some home remodeling to do.

Sue Fenton, Madison, referring to former Sheriff Fate Thomas using prisoners and government resources to remodel his home

You think the politician running for a four-year term can still be effective because he's only serving one to three.

Kent Chitwood, Nolensville

You think that a coming-out party is the celebration held when your favorite political candidate is released from prison.

Somer Hooker, Brentwood

Before placing a lost-and-found ad to find your pet, you check the Governor's Mansion first.

Robert Meyer, referring to the controversy when Governor Don Sundquist took in a child's lost dog

Your senator is a cat killer and your governor is a dog thief.

> *Hank Fincher, referring to Senator Bill Frist's revelation that*
> *he took in cats and practiced his medical school skills on them*

Your legislator cares more about what Darwin said about you than
what the rest of the country thinks about you.

> *Greg Denton, referring to the controversy over*
> *legislation requiring the teaching of Creationism*

GRIDIRON POLITICIANS

Probably more one-liners are delivered at Gridiron Dinners than at
any other political events. At these dinners, members of the news
media perform and entertain. The following are samples of their wit
and work, each a comment about a politician:

"He is so lazy he don't do nothing; and don't start that 'til noon!"[3]

"He approaches every issue with an open mouth."

"There's two sides to every question—and he takes both of 'em."

"If he said what was on his mind, he'd be speechless."

"There's two kinds of people in the world—and he ain't neither one
of 'em."

Davy Crockett: Tennessee's First Political Humorist

"One of the first yarn spinners in American politics, surpassed in fame only by Lincoln, was Davy Crockett, who used the yarn as he did the whiskey treat, to obtain votes," wrote a noted scholar of American humor.[1] To be ranked second only to the revered President Lincoln is high praise indeed. Sometimes, we are reminded that a prophet is without honor in his or her own home area. Perhaps that explains why some of us fail to appreciate fully just how talented and unique Crockett was. And like prophets, Crockett was ahead of his time and showed the way to many who followed.

David Crockett hailed from all across Tennessee. Born in 1786 in East Tennessee, he lived there his first twenty-seven years, except for about thirty months of what he called a "strategic withdrawal" as a teenager.[2]

He then lived a dozen years in three Middle Tennessee counties, where he volunteered for the Indian wars, became a local government official and a militia colonel, and was elected to the Tennessee House of Representatives. Defeated in a bid for a third legislative term, he moved again.

In West Tennessee, Crockett quickly became known as a champion bear hunter and taleteller. In 1827, he first won a race for the United States House of Representatives. He last represented West Tennessee in Congress in 1835, when he again lost a bid for reelection. He then headed to Texas and died at the Alamo in March of 1836.

Crockett was an extraordinarily humorous taleteller. He also was an amazingly effective campaigner, repeatedly winning elections, and narrowly losing two congressional races only because he dared oppose

Tennessee's Congressman David Crockett was elected and reelected in part on his fame as a frontiersman and champion bear hunter, mythologized as Davy Crockett. Tennessee State Library and Archives, Rose Music Collection.

the policies of Tennessee's own President Andrew Jackson. His entertaining taletelling and effective campaigning were not unrelated.

Frontier families were separated and isolated. They had little entertainment and few opportunities for social interaction. Barn buildings, house raisings, and harvests needed to be and were social events, times of play as well as hard work. As Crockett biographer James A. Shackford pointed out: "Political searches in the backwoods were no more to be divorced from entertainment, from tall tales, from picnic, frolic, barbecue, stomp-down, than freckles from a boy who lives in the sun. Woe be to the political candidate who did not know this need for entertainment or who, knowing it, could not cater to it naturally. This urgent need for social entertainment is also a practical explanation of the fact that the tall tale was *so* tall."[3]

Settlers living constantly in peril needed to joke about danger in order to release bursting tension. And so, Shackford maintains, "[T]he wonders were made *ridiculously* wonderful. Each hunter must out lie every other about the nature of the marvels which had personally befallen him," something that Crockett excelled in doing.[4]

Shackford states that "the politics of the frontier was the politics of the backwoodsmen." If a candidate could not entertain the pioneers, he could not gain their votes.[5]

Following are tales by and about David Crockett. Some of them may seem to take some space to unfold. And some may not strike the reader as being as funny as they were to Crockett's frontier listeners. Tastes in humor and entertainment have changed somewhat over almost two centuries. Still, Crockett set the mark. He was Tennessee's first political humorist and perhaps the nation's leading one. His reputation, example, and influence stretched far beyond our state and far beyond his time.

Several of the stories are not about politics, or at least at first do not seem to be. But even those tales were in Crockett's 1834 autobiography, *A Narrative of the Life of David Crockett of the State of Tennessee,* a book that became part of his congressional campaign. The book and its stories also played a role in his being promoted by the Whigs to run for president against Andrew Jackson's chosen successor, Martin Van Buren.[6]

Crockett's success and fame, as well as the effectiveness of his attacks on Jackson's policies, caused Jackson and other Crockett opponents to strive vigorously to beat him in the 1835 congressional election.[7] When Crockett lost that race, it effectively took him out of the 1836 presidential election. The defeat also took him out of Tennessee and sent him to Texas. The rest, as they say, is history. This history also includes no small amount of myth, since Crockett's life and exploits in Tennessee and Texas grew larger with his death and continued to grow for decades after. The following stories are either true or at least were told as true by Crockett himself.

NOT A BOY, NOR A GOAT

In 1813, settlers in Middle Tennessee fought with the Creeks. Crockett himself was living in Franklin County then. That fall, he signed up for the fight.

As the troops assembled, a Major Gibson was looking for volunteers to go scout the movements of the Creeks on the other side of the Tennessee River. Crockett was recommended for the expedition, accepted the opportunity, and was allowed to choose a companion. Crockett chose George Russell, the young son of an early settler of Franklin County whom Crockett knew.

Major Gibson objected that young Russell did not have beard enough and said he wanted men, not boys, for such a dangerous task. Crockett replied that if courage was measured by the beard, a goat would have preference over a man.

Young Russell was allowed to go with Crockett.

REPORTS OF CROCKETT'S DEATH

In the fall of 1816, Crockett and some neighbors explored the Alabama country, recently acquired from the Creeks, looking for a new place to settle. While exploring, Crockett suffered a severe attack of illness that may have been malaria. He was fortunate to survive, but eventually he returned home.

Crockett's reappearance astonished his home folks, for his original companions had returned long before him. So surely had they been convinced Crockett would die that when they returned his horse they exaggerated the story. They reported not only that they had left

Crockett dying, but also that they later talked to men who had seen him draw his last breath and had helped to bury him.

Concerning this report of his death, Crockett commented, "I know'd this was a whapper of a lie, as soon as I heard it."[8]

THE FATHER

David Crockett's first wife died, leaving him with young children. Before long he married Elizabeth Patton, a widow who also had young children. Historians report it was a "congenial marriage" and that the two families "came quite harmoniously together."[9]

Before long, Elizabeth gave birth to still more children. Later, when all the children engaged in a free-for-all, Crockett would shout to his wife, "Come Bess! Your children and my children are whippin' ———— out of our children!"

RUNNING FOR COLONEL

A Captain Matthews told Crockett that he was running for election as colonel of the 57th Militia Regiment of Lawrence County. Matthews urged Crockett to run with him, but for first major, with the idea of gaining Crockett's support for Matthews's own election as colonel. Crockett allegedly was reluctant to run, but finally agreed.

Later, Matthews had a "frolic" to gain support in the election. Crockett discovered Matthews was running his own son for the same first major's position which he had talked Crockett himself into seeking. Crockett pulled Matthews aside and got him to admit his son indeed was Crockett's opponent.

Matthews attempted to defend his double-dealing by saying that the son hated to run against Crockett worse than against any other man in the country. Crockett replied that the son need not worry about that, for Crockett had decided not to run for first major after all. Crockett assured Matthews he would not run against his son. Instead, Crockett vowed he would run against Matthews himself for colonel.

Matthews then displayed a more honorable side, as well as a sense of humor. Or maybe he just decided it was best to get the bad news out himself. In any event, Matthews got the attention of the crowd and announced that Crockett was to be his opponent.

Crockett then spoke and explained why he was running against their host. Crockett told what he had learned about the son running against him for major. Then he told the crowd that "as I had the whole family to run against any way, I was determined to levy on the head of the mess."[10]

Election day, Crockett beat the father. Matthews's son also lost.

THE LEGISLATIVE CANDIDATE

Crockett learned from observing his opponents. Specifically, he learned the power of making promises—including, and perhaps especially, the value of an ambivalent promise.

In 1821, while living in Lawrence County, Crockett ran for the Tennessee House of Representatives. He sought to represent Lawrence and Hickman Counties. One of the heated issues he encountered in Hickman County involved Vernon, a town that Crockett said wanted to be moved. Crockett claimed to be perplexed by how to move a town and what exactly citizens wanted. In fact, however, the issue was whether to move the county seat from Vernon to neighboring Centerville, an issue each town's inhabitants felt very strongly about.

In the course of campaigning, Crockett returned to Hickman County. He assured the people that he had been "thinkin' a lot about the problem, and was still mullin' it over," but had not yet come to a conclusion. He promised he would surely reach some conclusion before election day, and his conclusion would be right for all.

Historians report that this seemed fair, and "left both parties in a pleasant state of hope."[11]

THE CAMPAIGNER

In 1822, Crockett moved his family to West Tennessee. In February 1823, "a man came to my house and told me I was a candidate. I told him not so." The man took out a newspaper and showed Crockett where he had "announced." Crockett told his wife it was "a burlesque on me, but I was determined to make it cost the man who had put it in there at least the value of the printing, and of the fun he wanted at my expense." And Crockett started campaigning.

Crockett had a buckskin hunting shirt made with pockets large enough to hold a big twist of chewing tobacco and a bottle of liquor. After a prospective voter took a taste of "the *creature*," Crockett said he immediately handed the voter a replacement for the "chaw" he had to discard to take the drink. Thus, "he would not be worse off than when I found him; and I would be sure to leave him in a first-rate good humor."

THE BEAR HUNTER

In the 1820s, many bears still roamed northwest Tennessee. Crockett apparently was as effective as a bear hunter as he was as a candidate. Crockett reported that he (probably together with his hunting companions) in less than a year killed 105 bears.

Crockett's hunting experiences made for some humorous and tall tales. He used colorful details even in setting up the stories. For example, he told of a hunting expedition during which "[w]e had just eat our breakfast, when a company of hunters came to our camp, who had fourteen dogs, but all so poor, that when they would bark they would almost have to lean up against a tree and take a rest."

During the same hunting trip, Crockett managed to kill a bear, but then claimed to have encountered the following difficulties.

> I suffered very much that night with cold, as my leather breeches, and every thing else I had on, was wet and frozen. But I managed to get my bear out of this crack after several hard trials, and so I butchered him, and laid down to try to sleep. But my fire was very bad, and I couldn't find any thing that would burn well to make it any better; and I concluded I should freeze, if I didn't warm myself in some way by exercise. So I got up, and hollered a while, and then I would just jump up and down with all my might, and throw myself into all sorts of motions. But all this wouldn't do; for my blood was now getting cold, and the chills coming all over me. I was so tired, too, that I could hardly walk; but I thought I would do the best I could to save my life, and then, if I died, nobody would be to blame. So I went to a tree about two feet through, and not a limb on it for thirty feet, and I would climb up it to the limbs, and then lock my

arms together around it, and slide down to the bottom again. This would make the insides of my legs and arms feel mighty warm and good. I continued this till daylight in the morning, and how often I clomb up my tree and slid down I don't know, but I reckon at least a hundred times.

THE DEFEATED CANDIDATE'S EXPLANATION

Crockett ran for Congress in 1825. He came up short, a loss he explained this way:

> Providence was a little against two of us this hunt, for it was the year that cotton brought twenty-five dollars a hundred; and so Colonel Alexander [the incumbent Congressman] would get up and tell people, it was all the good effect of this tariff law; that it had raised the price of their cotton, and that it would raise the price of everything else they made to sell. I might as well have sung *salms* over a dead horse, as to try to make the people believe otherwise; for they knowed their cotton had raised, sure enough, and if the colonel hadn't done it, they didn't know what had. So he rather made a mash of me this time as he beat me exactly *two* votes. . . .[12]

CONGRESSIONAL CANDIDATE

Crockett told another tale from the congressional campaign trail. He said he had "started off to the Cross Roads, dressed in my hunting shirt, and my rifle on my shoulder."[13] He came upon a crowd listening to one of his opponents near a "shantee" tavern owned by a "gander-shanked Yankee." The crowd saw Crockett and called on him to speak. He "mounted the stump" and "began to bushwack in the approved style."

Soon the crowd let Crockett know they could not listen to him speak on such a dry topic as the nation's welfare without something to drink. Crockett then led the crowd into the tavern and ordered a quart of rum. The Yankee tavern owner, however, refused to serve the liquor because Crockett was unable to pay. The crowd quickly deserted Crockett. Crockett then took his rifle into the woods. In fifteen minutes he killed and skinned a coon.

He returned to the tavern, traded the skin for a quart of rum, resumed the stump, and recovered the crowd. When the rum was gone and the hearers again grew thirsty, Crockett had to lead them back into the shantee. He feared he would have to go shoot another coon. But Crockett spotted sticking between the logs that supported the bar the tail of the coonskin he had already used. Crockett pulled the coonskin out, slapped it on the counter, and got another quart.

"I wish I may be shot," claimed Crockett, "if I didn't before the day was over, get ten quarts for the same identical skin."

CONGRESSMAN CROCKETT'S FIRST SESSION

In 1827, Crockett was elected to the Twentieth Congress. He attended its first session in December 1827. Some months later a Tennessee newspaper reported Crockett claimed he was not afraid to address the United States House of Representatives because he could "whip any man in it." Furthermore, Crockett reportedly had come to Congress boasting he could "wade the Mississippi, carry a steamboat on his back, and whip his weight in wild-cats."

NAME CALLING

No issue was as important to Crockett as passing legislation that would let the settlers purchase the land they were living on and working. Others, however, wanted to protect land speculators instead of the settlers. Still others disagreed on how to achieve either goal.

One of Crockett's Tennessee colleagues in Congress was future President James K. Polk of Columbia. Crockett and Polk came to differ over how to proceed and the form of land claim legislation. Crockett was attacked and blamed as principally responsible for the defeat of Polk's land bill. One unnamed critic was reported in a newspaper to have written of Crockett: "He is estranged from his colleagues, associates chiefly with the other side, and has openly set himself up in market, offering to vote for anything in order to get votes by it."

Crockett exploded in reply:

> My vote in market!! I the cause of defeating a proposition for the benefit of my constituents?!!! The kindness of my feelings toward the human fam-

ily in general, would prompt me to give it some softer name, if I were not fully convinced that the author of this WICKED LIE, is some *contemptible wretch,* who seeks to gratify a secret feeling of revenge, which he dares not openly avow.

Crockett continued by calling the author of the charge a *"poltroon, a scoundrel,* and a *puppy,"* and saying that if he would "avow himself," Crockett "would condescend to take further notice of him."

YANKEE TEASING AND SOUTHERN WIT

The following story reveals New Englanders' initial attitude toward Crockett—and Tennessee. It also demonstrates Crockett's ability to defend both his state and himself.

In Washington, a Massachusetts congressman happened to see Congressman Crockett at the same time a farmer was driving some mules down Pennsylvania Avenue. The Massachusetts congressman called out: "Hello, there, Crockett, here's a lot of your constituents on parade. Where are they going?"

Crockett quickly replied: "They are going to Massachusetts to teach school."

ANOTHER CAMPAIGN

During a campaign, one Crockett opponent was a Colonel Cook, who repeatedly attacked Crockett. For every evil charge his opponent made against him, Crockett made a worse one against Colonel Cook. The adversary, knowing Crockett's charges were completely false, shrewdly planned to trap him. He arranged to face Crockett at the conclusion of one of Crockett's harangues with witnesses to prove Crockett had been lying. By catching Crockett in the act, Cook thought he could humiliate Crockett publicly and finish him politically.

When Crockett arose and spoke, Crockett seemed to outdo himself in making false charges. At the apparent conclusion of his speech, Crockett paused as if about to sit down. Then Crockett smiled, and he added that his opponent had brought witnesses to trap him and prove that Crockett had been spreading lies. Crockett said his opponent might have saved himself all the trouble by simply asking Crockett if he was lying about Colonel Cook, for he would have freely admitted he was. Crockett said he thought, however, he had as much right to lie about his competitor as his competitor had to lie about him—for they had *both* been lying all the time.

Anything Crockett's opponent and the witnesses might have said after Crockett's admission would have been superfluous and lost in the roar of the crowd. Crockett's adversary, "who had more justice than astuteness on his side, withdrew from the canvass in righteous indignation over the irrationality of the electorate, saying that he would not consent to represent people who would applaud an acknowledged liar."

THE BREAK WITH PRESIDENT JACKSON

In Crockett's words, his break with President Andrew Jackson "was considered the unpardonable sin," and he "was hunted down like a wild varment" by newspapers and "every little pin-hook lawyer."

One Jacksonian tactic was the use of "Black Hawk . . . [alias] Adam Huntsman, with all his talents for writing 'Chronicles.'" Adam Huntsman was a West Tennessee lawyer and politician of considerable shrewdness, and a local political writer of ingenuity and wit. He was a Jackson supporter and was finally to defeat Crockett for Congress in 1835. In 1833, he did not compete with Crockett directly, but he did have a shrewd hand in the effort to scotch Crockett's political wagon. His "Chronicles" attacked Crockett by impugning his motives in his fight for the land bill. Done in biblical language to which the wide use of Hebraic names in the backwoods gave great point, they combined humor and information in a way that must have counted heavily with Crockett's backwoods constituents.

A brief selection from these "Chronicles" gives the flavor of Huntsman's wit and presents the Jacksonian version of what was happening to Crockett:

> 1. And it came to pass in those days when Andrew was chief Ruler over the Children of Columbia, that there arose a mighty man in the river country whose name was David; he belonged to the tribe of Tennessee, which lay upon the border of the Mississippi and over against Kentucky. . . .
>
> 6. And it came to pass in the 54th year after the Children of the Columbia had escaped British bondage, and on the first month, when

Andrew and the wise men and rulers of the people were assembled in the great san hedrim, that David arose in the midst of them saying, men and brethren, wot ye not that there be many occupants in the river country on the west border of the tribe of Tennessee, who are settled down upon lands belonging to Columbia; now I beseech you give unto these men each a portion for his inheritance, so that his soul may be glad, and he will bless thee and thy posterity.

[But there were other "wise men" who objected, saying that the central government should give the land to Tennessee, who should in turn deal with the occupants—thus giving all Tennessee politicians, and, not just David, the glory for ever and ever. But David became angry at their resistance to his scheme and vowed vengeance. . . .]

9. Now there were in these days wicked men, sons of Belial, to wit: the Claytonites, the Holmesites, the Burgessites, the Everettites, the Chiltonites, and the Bartonites, who were of the tribes of Maine, Massachusetts, Rhode Island, Kentucky, and Missouri, and who hated Andrew and his friends of old times, because the Children of Columbia had chosen him to rule over them instead of Henry whose surname was Clay, whom they desired for their chief ruler.

[These "Sons of Belial" saw that David was angry at his own group and made advances to this man who had fought against their great chiefs Henry and John Q. Then Daniel, surnamed Webster, a "prophet of the Order of Balaam . . ."]

12. [D]rew nigh unto David and said unto him, Wherefore . . . doth thou seem sad and sorrowful? . . . And David lifted up his eyes and wept. . . .

THE LAST CAMPAIGN

During Crockett's last campaign, he and his opponent, Adam Huntsman, traveled the district together, and spoke, literally, from the same stumps. Huntsman, also known as "Black Hawk" for his pen name, had lost a leg in the Indian wars and walked with a wooden leg.

One evening Crockett and Huntsman both stayed with a prosperous and politically influential farmer who, though quite hospitable to both, was supporting Huntsman. The household eventually retired for the night, and the contenders for Congress stayed in the same room. After Huntsman went to sleep, Crockett lay figuring how to win the farmer's support.

This farmer had an attractive, young, and unmarried daughter.

At one end of the back porch was her room and at the other end was the room Crockett and Huntsman shared. That night, Crockett quietly arose and carried a chair across the porch to the young lady's door. Crockett then made noise as if trying to break into her room. The frightened young woman screamed. Crockett then placed one foot upon the rungs of the chair, hobbled quickly back across the wooden porch, closed the door, and jumped into bed. Still dressed for bed, Crockett pretended to be asleep.

Soon the farmer burst into the room and rudely awakened Adam Huntsman. The sleepy Huntsman claimed ignorance of what the farmer was yelling about and protested his innocence of anything but sleep. The outraged farmer would not be satisfied, for he knew he had distinctly heard Huntsman's wooden leg striking across the porch. Furthermore, the farmer knew Huntsman's reputation concerning women.

Crockett "awakened" just in time to stop the indignant father from harming the ingrate who had violated the hospitality of his home and sought to violate his daughter. Crockett eventually restored some order, and he even guaranteed Huntsman's proper behavior for the rest of the night. The farmer still roundly declared, in spite of Crockett's apparently generous efforts to appease him, that his vote now had been completely changed from Huntsman to Crockett, and he vowed he would change as many of his friends' votes as he could.

THE DEPARTURE

On a November night in 1835, Crockett engaged in a farewell drinking party in Memphis. Called upon for remarks, Crockett talked about the recent election, which he had lost by 252 votes. Noting that many who should have voted for him instead had voted for Adam Huntsman, Crockett concluded, "Since you have chosen to elect a man with a timber toe to succeed me, you may all go to ——— and I will go to Texas."

Pickin' Cotton:
Professional Political Humor

Since this chapter is full of tales by Cotton Ivy, it falls on me (Roy Herron) to introduce it. I am reminded of what Senator Jim Sasser once said of Cotton: "Cotton's idea of a seven-course meal is a possum and a six-pack."[1]

Cotton might respond, "If Jim Sasser's so smart, how come he's *former* Senator Sasser?"

But Jim Sasser is right about Cotton being "country." (As is his co-author, for sure.) Cotton has made his living with his mouth—his country mouth—for a lot of years. He also has served Tennessee in our House of Representatives and as our commissioner of agriculture. But before that, after that, and even during his stint of public service, he has told more tales than any Tennessean since Davy Crockett. He has made more people laugh than anybody conceived in this state since Samuel Clemens's parents got together while living in the Upper Cumberland and started what would become Mark Twain.

What follows is some of Cotton's best political humor. As you read, I think you will see why for a number of years so many organizations and outfits all over this country looking for a great speaker and a great time have been pickin' Cotton.

Unless noted otherwise, the following stories are from a tape called "Politics and Cotton." These stories were recorded during one of Cotton's performances in about 1986, while Cotton was a state representative.

PROUD TO BE A POLITICIAN

I'm proud to be a politician. Politicians smile. Do you know why we smile? Because we believe what Daniel Webster said when he said that one of the great joys of life is happiness in duty.

The Honorable L. H. "Cotton" Ivy appears here in a publicity photo before he became honorable. Or at least before he was elected to the Tennessee House of Representatives and was appointed commissioner of agriculture. Metropolitan Nashville Government Archives, *Nashville Banner* Collection.

And we believe that we are performing our duty when we serve our fellow human beings, and you folks believe the same thing, and that's why you're happy in doing what you do.

Of course after you get in politics, you change a little bit. My mama said, "Son, you get you a speech and you memorize it and you run your mouth until you get elected, and then you learn to keep that mouth shut sometimes after you get elected."

POLITICIAN TALK

I have learned to talk a little bit different after I have been in the legislature. Before you could ask me, "Cotton, what is two plus two?" and I would say, "four." But now you ask me, "What is two plus two?" and I might say: "If by human chance you find it necessary to add the numerator of the second denomination to the figure two, the result will always be, and I say this without fear of contradiction, because it is an absolute, the result will always be four."

You just learn to elaborate, like lawyers do sometimes.

RUNNING YOUR PEDIGREE

If you don't want your pedigree run, if you don't want your family tree looked up, you don't need to hop out there in politics. Somebody will do it for you—for free.

In one of the four counties I represent, I knew a fellow runnin' for a courthouse position. After two weeks he put a notice in the paper. He said, "I'm quittin'." He said, "I'm finished. My name is on the ballot, but I'm through."

I saw him, and I said, "Bill, looked like it was goin' all right. Why'd you quit, son?"

He said, "Well, let me tell you, they started tellin' everything on me. You can't believe what all lies they was tellin' on me. And Cotton, the reason I quit was that, some of them lies they was tellin' on me, they can really prove!"

A DOUBTFUL VOTE

When you kiss a baby, and the mama grabs a wash rag and washes that baby's face right quick, you need to mark that vote down as "doubtful."

WHO KNEW HE HAD IT IN HIM?

A candidate came down to our courthouse makin' him a talk, and he shelled the corn down—talkin' about motherhood, patriotism, and two chickens in every pot. And the mayor got up there. He was for that candidate. The mayor said, "What a beautiful speech! What a great oration! Who among us knew he had it in him?"

Cuckleburr got up and said, "Yes sir, I knew he had it in him. Before he got up there to talk, in the rest room I saw him drink it every drop."

THE HONEST CANDIDATE

I remember one candidate ended up his speech and then said he'd be glad to answer any questions. He was asked about campaign finance reform and illegal contributions. He scratched his head a bit, then came up with his position on this perplexing issue: "Well, I'll tell you one thing. If I'm ever caught with any illegal campaign contributions, I'll return them immediately."

A DOG AND A CUCKLEBURR

Every politician has a relationship with dogs, be it good or bad. And I'm no exception. I'm a dog man. I appreciate dogs. I was campaignin' last election. I called on a farmer. He had an old coon dog tied out there where you could see him, and I couldn't hardly talk to him for that old dog hollerin'. And I'd try to say another word, and he'd holler again. And I finally said, "Sir, what's wrong with that dog?"

He said, "Oh, he's just settin' on a cuckleburr."

I said, "Well, why don't he move?"

He said, "He's a politician dog. He'd rather holler than do anything about it."

A PROFESSIONAL POLITICIAN DOG

I ran into a professional politician dog. Me and my brother was out campaignin'. I got him to ride with me. We came up on this house, and I knocked on the door. And usually you will hear a little lapdog holler, but this was a great big dog. I identified myself: "Hello, this is Cotton Ivy. I'm runnin' for the state legislature—I wanna politic with you a little bit."

About that time that fella' opened that door, and that dog came on me. Attacked me. I started to run, threw my campaign cards up in the air tryin' to get back to the pickup. That dog grabbed me. Bit me on the calf of the leg. I finally got in the truck and when I did, I saw my brother going around the pickup. Dog grabbed him and bit him on the heel. The fella on the porch was calling, "Come here, Joe! Whoa, Joe, here, come here, Joe!" He finally got a leash on Old Joe.

Fella said, "I'm sorry about this, but that dog is a professional trained dog against politicians. And when he heard you say you were a politician, there was nothing I could do about it—you set him on fire."

I said, "Well, I can understand that's why he bit me, but why did he bite my *brother* who ain't got nothin' to do with politics?"

He said, "Sir, he hates politicians so bad that when he bites one, he has to bite somebody else right quick to get the taste out of his mouth."

YORE DOG BITE?

Another time I was out campaigning by myself and saw an old boy settin' on the porch whittling.

Whittling is a big thing where I come from. A man who won a whittling contest last year had a knife so sharp he got a gallon of shavings off a kitchen match. That knife was so sharp that a shadow fell off that knife and cut a man's walking stick right in half.

That old boy was up there whittling on a piece of red cedar, old wooly booger dog laying out there in the yard. I saw him. Walked up there in about three feet of him. Old dog stood up, every tooth in his head shining, hair on him wrong side out. I stopped. I looked at the fellow on the porch. He never did look up.

I said, "Hey, Mister, does yore dog bite?"

He never did look up. Just said, "Naw."

I took another step and that old dog started toward me. Gnarling and biting at me all the way down the hill, me backing, never turned my back on him. Dog right in front of me gnarling.

When I got to my pickup, I rolled the window down and said, "Hey, Mister, I thought you said your dog don't bite."

Old boy never looked up. He just said, "That ain't my dog."

PORE COTTON'S CHILDHOOD

Every politician likes to talk about the poverty-stricken areas they came from and the days they were poor. I heard one governor tell about how he was born in a log cabin he built with his own hands! Politicians exaggerate.

But I want you to know that it is authentic when I tell you that I came from poor country. That I represent counties that are still poor. That I came from a poor family. In a poverty-stricken area.

The only black dirt we've got is where we changed the oil in them old pickups and tractors.

We have to plant three peas at a time—one push and one pull—to get one up.

We did not live off income. We lived off a lack of expenses.

I want you to know this here politician was probably one of the poorest politicians that ever lived. My Daddy cut a picture out of a magazine of a ham of meat and pasted it on the dining room table and got him a two-pound slab of fatback—that's middlin' pork—and slung it with a wire about two feet above our dining room table. Us children would come in and set down around the dinin' room table, and Pappy would come in and swing that fatback, back and forth, and us children would sop the shadow.

You see, I was born durin' the Depression, not the recession. I know what rabbit sausage tastes like without anything mixed in it.

And we didn't have shotgun shells to kill a rabbit with either. We'd have to run that rabbit until he got tired and went in a hole in the ground or climbed up in a hollow tree. And then we'd go cut us a big long stick and slice the end of it and we'd run that stick up in that hole where that rabbit was and we'd start twistin' and turnin' it to the right and twistin' and those rabbits got smart, and they started turnin' to the right the way we were twistin' and it got hard to get rabbits.

But there was a left-handed boy moved into that community that nearly cleaned that country out of rabbits before they caught onto what he was doin'.

HELPING THIS STRICKEN AREA

Politicians learn to think fast on their feet. We had a candidate who came down to Tywop and he said, "What can I do to help this stricken area if I'm elected?"

And Uncle Eb said, "Well, I can tell you what you can do. You can take from the rich and give to us poor folks. Do like Robin Hood did. That's what you can do."

And the politician was a fast thinker. Said, "Even if we did that, it wouldn't be but a year or two 'til the wealthy and the affluent would have all the wealth back again."

Uncle Eb said, "Not the way I'm suggestin'. I'm talking about dividin' up every Saturday evenin'."

POLITICAL WINDS BLOWING

In the midst of an election every candidate claims his political wind is blowin'. We try to conjure up a storm when it's a gentle breeze. We exaggerate about our political wind.

An analyst once wrote on a speech a fellow gave: "High wind, big thunder, no rain." A lot of times that's so.

Politicians are not the only ones who exaggerate about the wind. We entertain ourselves by exaggeration in the country, and it's expected. But you could tell I was a-headed into politics by some of my family and the tales they tell. Down at Buddy's Grocery we'd had a big wind the night before, and I was down there next morning. A few pieces of tin blown up, few shingles, no big deal. But they were talking wind. And Uncle Jimmy said: "Last night wadn't nothin. My daddy said he saw wind blow a thirty-five foot log chain out of a wagon bed that had sideboards on it. Said he saw that."

Uncle Fred punched me, and he said: "Well, that ain't nothin'.

I've got relatives in East Tennessee said the wind blowed so hard one night that next morning there was a thirty gallon iron wash kettle blowed wrong-side-out, legs on the inside."

Uncle Sy said, "Well, didn't nobody see that, that was at night, wasn't it?" Uncle Fred said, "Yes." Uncle Sy said: "Well, I saw this with my own eyes. A streak of hard wind come through my place, picked up an eight-pound rooster, blowed him in a small-mouth gallon jug. And blowed an iron anvil across my yard, and blowed it so fast lightnin' struck at it twice—missed it both times."

Uncle Eb is the store's proprietor. He's gonna be the biggest and the best. After all the laughin' and gigglin' ceases, he's going to talk. He said: "Folks, I guess I saw the wind blow harder than a human being ever saw. There was a suckin', twistin' wind come through my place, blowed a fifty foot well plum out of the ground. I turned it upside down, painted it white and used it for a silo. Look out that window right there."

A VULNERABLE, LOST POLITICIAN

There are times during a politician's life when he is vulnerable. When he is runnin' for election or reelection. One candidate described it as: "We must endure the voter's wit." In other words, the voter can say pretty well what he or she wants to you at that time. And I have found it that way out on the campaign trail.

I was in an area in one of the counties that I did not frequent. Not many folks lived up there. Houses were so far apart everybody had their own tomcat. Those of you that are country will understand what I mean. I came around a curve, and there was a fellow settin' on the porch, and I was lost. I was going to try to ease into tryin' to find my way back to town.

I said, "How do you get to town, Old-timer?"

He said, "Usually takes two of us. One of us knows the way down there and the other one knows the way back."

I said, "Have you lived here all your life, Old-timer?"

He said, "Not yet."

I said, "I'm really lookin' for directions. Where does this road go?"

He said, "I've lived here a long time. Every mornin' when I get up, the road's right there. Don't go nowhere."

I said, "You don't understand what I'm talkin' about. I'm trying to get to Sugar Tree and the road's forked. Which road do I take?"

He said, "Now, you can't take neither one of them. Both of them belong to the government, far as I know."

And I just kind of lost my patience, and I said, "You're about a half-smart alec. Don't have a whole lot of sense, do you?"

He said, "Well, son, I ain't lost."

KUDZU CONTROL

We learn something from every election. Last election in Tennessee we learned how to control kudzu.

Are y'all familiar with that climbin' vine? Grows so fast it can wrap around your leg while you're standin' there.

We learned how to control it. Take that black-labeled Jack Daniel's and pour it on that kudzu and some politician will *gnaw it out by the roots.*

THE GOVERNMENT MAN AND UNCLE EB
ON MAKIN' ALCOHOL

A government man came in and was goin' to teach us how to produce home-grown alcohol. Uncle Eb said he wanted to be legal one time in his life. He was sittin' on the front seat at the courthouse. After ten minutes it was obvious that he knew more than the government man. So the government man looked at him and said: "Sir, what do you think about mixin' your 200-proof product with gasoline? What do you think the effect will be?"

Uncle Eb said, "Well, it's going to hurt the taste, I know that."

The government man said, "What does it taste like now?"

Uncle Eb said, "Sir, did you ever swallow a coal oil lamp, and it lit?"

The government man's eyes got big. Uncle Eb went on: "It's strong. Folks have said that it's stouter than battery acid, and you need an asbestos mouth to drink it."

UNCLE EB'S FIRST VISIT TO THE LEGISLATURE

The first time that Uncle Eb came to the Tennessee legislature, he was sitting up in the gallery. That day happened to be a pretty lively session, with several legislators speaking at some length and with considerable passion. Someone sitting next to Uncle Eb finally asked him: "What do you think about it?"

Uncle Eb, having concluded that most every legislator seemed to have a pretty good-sized ego, said: "Well, all them politicians down there remind me of a log floatin' down the Tennessee River with hundreds of ants on that log. And every ant thinks he's drivin' that log."

UNCLE JOE'S TWO FINE BOYS

Uncle Joe was boasting about his sons. He said, "I've got two fine boys and I'm mighty proud of them. Neither of them has ever been in the penitentiary or the legislature."

Notes

INTRODUCTION

1. Proverbs 17:22, KJV.

2. Carroll Van West, ed., *The Tennessee Encyclopedia of History and Culture* (Nashville: Tennessee Historical Society, 1998).

3. Paul H. Bergeron, Stephen V. Ash, and Jeanette Keith, *Tennesseans and Their History* (Knoxville: Univ. of Tennessee Press, 1999).

4. Robert E. Corlew, *Tennessee: A Short History,* 2d ed. (Knoxville: Univ. of Tennessee Press, 1981).

5. John R. Vile and Mark Byrnes, eds., *Tennessee Government and Politics: Democracy in the Volunteer State* (Nashville, Tenn.: Vanderbilt Univ. Press, 1998).

6. William R. Majors, *The End of Arcadia: Gordon Browning and Tennessee Politics* (Memphis: Memphis State Univ. Press, 1982), 212.

7. We should note that there are precedents for this practice throughout Tennessee history. In his autobiography, for instance, David Crockett also substituted terminology. See David Crockett, *A Narrative of The Life of David Crockett of the State of Tennessee* (1834; reprint, Knoxville: Univ. of Tennessee Press, 1973), 168.

1. STATEWIDE ELECTIONS

1. Similarly, David Crockett once persuaded an opponent in a legislative race, Dr. Butler, to let him speak first. Crockett had heard Dr. Butler's speech many times. When Crockett took the stump, he gave Butler's speech verbatim, leaving his opponent speechless. See Herbert Harper, ed., *Houston and Crockett: Heroes of Tennessee and Texas: An Anthology* (Nashville: Tennessee Historical Commission, 1986), 148. Incidentally, Crockett's methods paid off in victory. On Sept. 16, 1823, he joined the Fifteenth General Assembly at Murfreesboro.

2. Joseph Bruce Gorman, *Kefauver: A Political Biography* (New York: Oxford University Press, 1971), 47–52; quotation on 47.

3. Ibid., 47.

4. Ibid., 48–49.

5. Ibid., 51.

6. The name has been changed to protect the guilty.

7. At a joint meeting of the House and Senate Judiciary Committees, Democratic Senator Steve Cohen took a partisan teasing shot at Republican Representative Randy Stamps. It was during a discussion of a new federal mandate, required by the Republican Congress, that child support go through Nashville instead of directly from the local clerk to the beneficiary. I volunteered: "I must come to the defense of my friend, Representative Stamps. He warned me in October of 1994, right before the election, that if I voted for Jim Sasser and Jim Cooper, then we would see more federal mandates imposed on us from Washington. Well, I voted for Congressman Jim Cooper and Senator Jim Sasser, and sure enough, he was right." Of course, in that election Bill Frist and Fred Thompson won over Senator Jim Sasser and Congressman Jim Cooper in the Republican landslide that gave them control of both houses of Congress (Roy Herron, personal experience, June 1998).

2. LOCAL ELECTIONS

1. The names have been changed to protect the guilty.

2. Former Lieutenant Governor Frank Gorrell was a key fundraiser for Congressman Al Gore Jr. when he ran for the United States Senate. Gorrell delivered a version of this speech in 1984 in Jackson, Tennessee, at a meeting of supporters working on a fundraising event for Congressman Gore.

3. LEGISLATIVE BRANCH: THE UNHOLY TRINITY

1. Robert A. Caro, *The Path to Power,* vol. 1 of *The Years of Lyndon Johnson* (New York: Knopf, 1982), 46–47.

2. West, *Tennessee Encyclopedia*, 122.

3. Majors, *The End of Arcadia,* 145.

4. Ibid.

5. Ibid., 146.

6. Numerous sources, including former Representative John Bragg and other legislators, report Cummings saying this. Another source is General Michael Catalano, *"Kidd v. McCanless:* The Genesis of Reappointment Litigation in Tennessee," *Tennessee Historical Quarterly* 44 (Spring 1985): 72. Catalano observes that the revenue collection and distribution numbers supported Mr. Cummings's statement, since his home county, Cannon, in 1958 collected $73,875.60 in state revenue while receiving $481,263.72 in state funds. Davidson County, by contrast, that same year collected $29,850.807.67 and received $4,409,038.94 in state funds. Some of the disparity, even in 1958, was due to rural citizens' trading in the cities.

7. Incidentally, Mister Jim took delight in the story. When others tell it, he said, they often make him the victim instead of his brother Clarence. "Somebody got the story out that it was me," Cummings said. "I've been asked twenty times. I said, "——— no, that was my brother. That wasn't me. I'd a remember the trial" (Billy Bowles and Remer Tyson, *They Love a Man in the Country* [Memphis, Tenn.: Peachtree, 1989]), 16.

4. LEGISLATIVE BRANCH: WHAT MAKES YOU THINK THEY READ THE BILLS?

1. Pat Miller, the source for this anecdote, was the aide whom Lieutenant Governor Wilder sent to talk with Representative Rhinehart. Hickory Withe was the community made famous in the litigation and the controversy that arose after legislation was adopted. That legislation surprised some when it dramatically changed the law on annexation in ways that went far beyond Hickory Withe.

5. EXECUTIVE BRANCH

1. Majors, *The End of Arcadia,* 148.
2. Ibid., 152.
3. Ibid., 234.
4. Veteran reporter Larry Daughtrey of Nashville's *Tennessean* notes he heard another reporter tell the same story, but involving Governor Prentice Cooper instead of Governor Clement. Pointing to Clement, however, is the fact that in 1954 he got his second highest percentage of votes in Johnson County, the county where Mountain City is located.
5. Gleason businessman Clay Wilson was telling why his friend, Speaker McWherter, would be elected governor in 1986. Wilson was right.
6. "He knew exactly what he was doing, too," McWherter aide Billy Stair laughingly recalled.

6. JUDICIAL BRANCH

1. Justice William H. D. Fones, "In Honor of Joseph W. Henry: The Best of Joe," *Tennessee Law Review* (Summer 1980): 681–87.
2. Ibid.
3. Fred Travis, "Justice Joe Henry's Sense of Humor," *Chattanooga Times,* 14 June 1980, D-3.
4. Ibid.
5. Seagram's and 7-Up, explained by Justice Henry in a footnote to his published opinion.
6. Thomas L. Peacock, "The Misfortunes of Elphinu."

7. "A Tribute to the Memory of Honorable John S. Wilkes," 199 Tenn. 745–55. See also "Memorial to the Honorable Joseph W. Henry," 624 S.W. 2d xxxvii–xl; Kirk Loggins, "Henry-Court's Social Conscience," *Nashville Tennessean,* 10 June 1980, 1, 6. Henry joined the U.S. Army in 1941 as a private and was discharged as a major in 1945. He became adjutant general in 1953. He received federal recognition as a major general in 1956.

8. Humorous reported decisions, including some from Tennessee, are found in: Wilmore Brown, ed., *The Legal Architect* (Charlottesville, Va.: Michie, 1959). Another book including opinions by Justice Wilkes is John B. McClay and Wendy L. Matthews, eds., *Corpus Juris Humorous* (New York: Macmillan/ McGraw-Hill, 1991). Collections of humorous stories about the law, as distinguished from court opinions, include John G. May, Jr., *The Lighter Side of the Law* (Charlottesville, Va.: Michie, 1956) and J. C. McMurty, *Humor in Tennessee Justice* (Tompkinsville, Ky.: Monroe County Press, 1979).

Tennessee's leading legal humorist, William H. Haltom Jr. of Memphis, has just published a book of humor called *In Search of Hamilton Burger: The Trials and Tribulations of a Southern Lawyer* (Nashville, Tenn.: Tennessee Bar Association Press, 2000). Author Roy Herron thinks Bill Haltom is the best humorist writing in Tennessee, period. He would think so even if Haltom were not the natural father of Will Haltom, Herron's godson.

9. *Southern Railway Company v. Phillips,* 42 S.W. 925, 100 Tenn. 130 (1897). This case refers to the case *Lyons v. Stills,* 37 S.W. 280, 97 Tenn. 514 (1896).

10. Judge Ben H. Cantrell, Tennessee Court of Appeals, in a letter dated Mar. 8, 1985, observed, "*Southern Ry.* was from James County which itself gave up the ghost shortly thereafter." James County was consolidated into Hamilton County in 1919, the first county consolidation in the United States, according to the *Tennessee Blue Book,* 1991–94 ed., 336.

11. Justice Wilkes wrote, it should be noted, about a century before the Tennessee Supreme Court had the benefit of Justice Martha Craig Daughtrey, the first woman on that court. It is not known what difference, if any, Justice Wilkes thought there was in "shooing" of men and women, or whether he thought men were too lazy to shoo chickens, or whether he thought men too insensitive to the beauty of flowers. It should be noted, however, that Justice Wilkes's great-granddaughter, Sylvia Sanders Kelley, reports that he rose to the bench in part because of his excellent advocacy on behalf of women.

12. A legal term meaning to take back by writ of replevin. A replevin is the recovery of goods or chattel claimed to be wrongfully taken or detained upon the person's giving security to try the matter in court and return the goods or chattel if defeated in the action.

13. This and other stories about Chancellor Brown should not be mis-understood to indicate a lack of respect for this enormously talented and exceptionally kind gentleman who was a dear friend of so many, includ-ing the authors.

14. For the benefit of other urban dwellers, it might need to be noted that a shoat is a young, weaned pig.

7. NATIONAL GOVERNMENT

1. The other was Senate Majority Leader Lyndon Baines Johnson of Texas.

2. Al Bissell's pronunciation was "Senatooor" and "Chiner."

8. ONE-LINERS

1. The Industrial Impact Subcommittee of the House of Representa-tives individually rekilled six TennCare bills and four other bills that McWherter ally Representative Shelby Rhinehart (D-Spencer) had killed the week before in one sweeping motion.

2. All of these answers are repeated in Dobie, *You Are So Nashville If,* on the following pages: Robertson, 45; Steel, 12; Fenton, 33; Chitwood, 29; Hooker, 57; Meyer, 139; Fincher, 126; Denton, 171.

3. This comment and the following ones to the end of the chapter were related by Terry Keeter in a speech in Memphis at a gridiron dinner, Apr. 1996.

9. DAVY CROCKETT

1. Charles Neider, ed., *The Comic Mark Twain Reader* (New York: Doubleday, 1977), xvii.

2. Crockett, *Narrative.* Crockett's work was one of the earliest autobiog-raphies, first published in 1834, only a decade and half after Ben Franklin's original. It also was perhaps the first example of Southwest humor, pub-lished only a year after the first of the Yankee type. See also Michael A. Lofaro, "Crockett, David 'Davy,'" *Tennessee Encyclopedia,* ed. West, 219–20.

3. James Shackford, *David Crockett: The Man and the Legend,* (Lincoln: Univ. of Nebraska Press, 1956), 242.

4. Ibid.

5. Ibid., 130. Shackford also maintains that "[p]ractical needs of pio-neer life required a healthy give and take: good sportsmanship was a fun-damental requisite of the political candidate. He had to have the ability not only to deliver an opponent a fierce blow by fist or anecdote, but also to accept with a smile a similar blow in return. In his early career, David had this ability. Hate came to be his undoing, and it destroyed his resilience."

6. Crockett himself obviously was looking forward to a run for the White House. See *Narrative,* 124, 131.

7. David Crockett's sense of humor was one reason he was perhaps more emblematic of the spirit of Jacksonian democracy than even Jackson himself. See *Narrative,* xi.

8. Crockett's comment reminds us of Mark Twain's comment that reports of his death were "greatly exaggerated." Note, however, that Twain (Samuel Langhorne Clemens) was born in 1835, the year before Crockett died. Twain clearly could have known of Crockett's humor, but not the other way around. As Charles Neider points out, "Mark Twain benefited consciously and thoroughly from the work of his predecessors. . . ." Neider specifically lists and quotes Crockett as one of Twain's predecessors. See his *The Comic Mark Twain Reader* (New York: Doubleday, 1977), xvii–xix.

9. Crockett was left with three children. Elizabeth herself had two children. Together, they had four more children.

10. See also Crockett, *Narrative,* 137–38. This election apparently was in 1818, since Crockett was commissioned on Mar. 27, 1818.

11. See also ibid., 142.

12. Crockett's defeat was narrow, but more than two votes.

13. Harper, *Houston and Crockett,* 159. At its beginning the anecdote was identified with the election of 1825, "when I first run for Congress." But Crockett was defeated in 1825. By the end of the account, its application had changed to the 1827 campaign, when he was successful. Crockett thus could claim his tactic at the tavern helped him win the election.

1O. PICKIN' COTTON

1. Speech by Jim Sasser, Oct. 1988.

Sources

1. STATEWIDE ELECTIONS

Note: The titles of the stories in this collection are the inventions of the authors of this book.

"Tennessee's War of the Roses" is from James Ewing, *A Treasury of Tennessee Tales* (Nashville, Tenn.: Rutledge Hill Press, 1985), 39–41.

"More Rose Wars" is from Ewing, *A Treasury of Tennessee Tales,* 40, 42.

"Governor Ben Hooper" is from Everett Robert Boyce, ed., *The Unwanted Boy: The Autobiography of Governor Ben W. Hooper* (Knoxville: Univ. of Tennessee Press, 1963), 65.

"Kefauver's Name Problem" is from Cotton Ivy, personal experience, 1948.

"Kefauver and Crump" is from Joseph Bruce Gorman, *Kefauver: A Political Biography* (New York: Oxford Univ. Press, 1971), 47–52.

"Boss Crump and Governor Browning" is from "Ed Crump, 'Master of the Put-down' and How He Did It to Gov. Browning," *Tennessee Town and City,* 11 May 1987, 6.

"Honest Elections" is from William Majors, *The End of Arcadia* (Memphis: Memphis State Univ. Press, 1982), 171–72.

"Governor Dunn's Preelection Fight" is from Lamar Alexander, *Steps Along the Way* (Nashville, Tenn.: Thomas Nelson, 1986), 36–37.

"Alexander's Walk across Tennessee" is from Alexander, *Steps Along the Way,* 15–16.

"Bulldog Ashe versus Al Gore" is from Tipton Country registrar, as told to Roy Herron, Aug. 1984.

"Candidate McWherter's Quick Stop" is from Charles G. Todd, as told to Roy Herron, 1987.

"Sign Problems" is from Charles G. Todd, as told to Roy Herron, 1999.

"Sleeping Tight Tonight" is from Charles G. Todd, as told to Roy Herron, Nov. 1999.

"They Warned Me" is from U.S. Senator James Sasser, speech delivered at Lane College, Jackson, 22 Oct. 1992.

"The Card-Playing Dog" is from Houston Gordon, speech delivered at the Hermitage Hotel, Nashville, June 1996.

2. LOCAL ELECTIONS

"The Spoils of Victory" is from U.S. District Judge Tom Wiseman, speech delivered at West End United Methodist Church, Nashville, 1988.

"My Dad Being an Election Official" is from Cotton Ivy, as told by his father, Howard Ivy, 1980.

"Double-Crossed" is from Joe Hill, as told to Roy Herron, 1995.

"Brawn and Brains" is from Ewing, *It Happened in Tennessee,* 142.

"The Sheriff's Reelection" is from Joe Hill, as told to Roy Herron, 1996.

"Ross Bass's Beating—and Winning" is from William H. Frist and J. Lee Annis Jr., *Tennessee Senators* (New York: Madison Books, 1999), 127.

"Representative Tommy Burnett" is from Cleve Smith, as told to Roy Herron, Feb. 1989.

"Another Burnett Story" is from Representative Tommy Burnett, as told to Roy Herron, Oct. 1989.

"Republican Puppies for Sale" is from Roy Auvenshine, speech delivered to McKenzie Lions Club, fall 1986.

"First One Seen Up Close" is from Senator Bobby Carter, letter to Roy Herron, Nov. 1999.

"Campaign Sign Destruction" is from Charles G. Todd, as told to Roy Herron, Nov. 1999.

"A County Executive's Political Advice" is from Andy Smith, as told to Cotton Ivy, 1990.

"Whiskey Speech" is from N. S. Sweat Jr., speech, copyright C-6101, 4 Apr. 1952.

"Representative Garrett on People Not Voting" is from Representative Tim Garrett, as told to Roy Herron, Oct. 1999.

"Prayerful Endorsements" is from *Tennessee Journal,* 19 Oct. 1998, 4.

3. LEGISLATIVE BRANCH: THE UNHOLY TRINITY

"Taking Care of Home-Folks" is from Majors, *The End of Arcadia,* 146.

"In the Penitentiary" is from Billy Bowles and Remer Tyson, *They Love a Man in the Country* (Atlanta, Ga.: Peachtree Publishers, 1989), 15–16.

"Representative I. D. Beasley and Governor Cooper" is from Bowles and Tyson, *They Love a Man in the Country,* 18.

"I. D. Beasley and the Hard-of-Hearing D. A." is from Bowles and Tyson, *They Love a Man in the Country,* 20.

"I. D. Beasley's Vote and Pete Haynes" is from Bowles and Tyson, *They Love a Man in the Country,* 20.

The Unholy Trinity and the Unholy Preacher" is from Bowles and Tyson, *They Love a Man in the Country,* 22–23.

"Finding the Capitol" is from Bowles and Tyson, *They Love a Man in the Country,* 28–29.

"Special License Plates and Spotted Horses" is from Bowles and Tyson, *They Love a Man in the Country,* 36.

"Jim Cummings in His Eighties" is from Bowles and Tyson, *They Love a Man in the Country,* 38.

4. LEGISLATIVE BRANCH: WHAT MAKES YOU THINK THEY READ THE BILLS?

"As If Bachelorhood Were Not Stressful Enough" is from an article in the *UT Torchbearer* (University of Tennessee alumni magazine) (Spring 1987).

"Suffrage and Motherhood" is from Ewing, *It Happened in Tennessee,* 132–37.

"Welcome to the Legislature" is from Tom Humphrey, as told to Roy Herron, Jan. 1999.

"Chairman Bragg's Meetings" is from Cotton Ivy, personal recollection.

"House Judiciary" is from *Tennessee Journal,* 4 Apr. 1994, 4.

"Judiciary Beanpickers" is from Tom Humphrey, "Notebook," *Knoxville News-Sentinel,* 30 Apr. 1995.

"Bewley's Moving Bills" is from Representative Art Swann, as told to Roy Herron, Aug. 1989.

"More Bewley Maneuvering" is from Roy Herron, personal recollection, Apr. 1988.

"The Buck Bewley Exception" is from Art Swann, as told to Roy Herron, Aug. 1988.

"The Liars Contest—More Bewley and Rhinehart" is from Tom Humphrey, as told to Roy Herron, Jan. 1999.

"Representative Rhinehart's Annexation Problem" is from Pat Miller, as told to Roy Herron, Jan. 1999.

"Rhinehart's Reelection Reflections" is from Cotton Ivy, personal recollection, Oct. 1999.

"Representative Rhinehart's Bodyguard" is from Representative Charles Curtiss, as told to Roy Herron, Oct. 1999.

"Beer and Dynamite" is from *Tennessee Journal,* 4 Apr. 1994, 4.

"Burnett and New Understandings" is from Representative Tommy Burnett, as told to Roy Herron and Cotton Ivy, Oct. 1999.

"Moving Bills" is from Roy Herron and Cotton Ivy, personal recollections.

"The Exploding Microphone" is from Cotton Ivy and Roy Herron, personal recollections.

"Casket Legislation Comes Alive in House Debate" is from Duren Cheek, "Casket Legislation Comes Alive in House Debate," *Nashville Tennessean,* 7 Mar. 1996.

"Banking and Cockfighting" is from Representative Ralph Cole, letter to Cotton Ivy, Oct. 1999.

"Representative Yard Boy" is from Representative Mike Williams, as told to Roy Herron, Oct. 1999.

"Dale Allen and the Newspaper Photo" is from Roy Herron, personal recollection, 1990.

"Work of Two Men" is from Roy Herron, personal recollection, Sept. 1997.

"Early Birds and Early Worms" is from Representative Ronnie Cole, speech to Northwest Tennessee Chambers of Commerce, Jan. 1999.

"Touchdowns and Paperwads" is from Roy Herron, personal experience, 1998.

"Representative Rinks's Introduction" is from Representative Randy Rinks, as told to Roy Herron, Oct. 1999.

"The Twilight Zone" is from Lieutenant Governor John S. Wilder, as told to Roy Herron, Feb. 1998.

"Wilder and the Preacher Lobbyist" is from Alexander, *Steps Along the Way,* 111–12.

"Speaker McWherter Flying with Speaker Wilder" is from Lieutenant Governor John S. Wilder, as told to Roy Herron, Oct. 1998.

"A President as Receptionist for Speaker McWherter" is from Larry Daughtery, as told to Roy Herron, Dec. 1999.

"Sam Donaldson and the Hillbilly Speaker" is from Larry Daughtery, as told to Roy Herron, Dec. 1999.

"Chairman Cooper" is from "Cooper's 4th District Bid Gives Business Lobbies Headache," *Nashville Tennessean,* 22 June 1998, 1, and from Roy Herron, personal recollection.

"Lieutenant Governor Frank Gorrell's Tick Johnson" is from Walter Durham, speech to Tennessee Historical Society, Oct. 1989.

"Senator Rochelle's Teddy Roosevelt Story" is from Senator Bob Rochelle, Feb. 1998.

"Senator Womack's Daughter's Phone Call" is from Senator Andy Womack, as told to Roy Herron, 1990.

"Whose Friend?" is from Milton Hamilton, as told to Roy Herron, Mar. 1991.

"Ducks and Gators" is from Milton Hamilton, as told to Roy Herron, Mar. 1991.

"Speaking Here Tonight" is from Roy Herron, personal experience, May 1997.

"The Black Poodle Hat" is from Cotton Ivy, personal recollection.

5. EXECUTIVE BRANCH

"Governor Hooper's Past—and Tennessee's Future" is from Boyce, *The Unwanted Boy,* 78.

"Governor Hooper on Governor Patterson" is from Boyce, *The Unwanted Boy,* 103.

"Governor Hooper's Boy" is from Boyce, *The Unwanted Boy,* 161.

"Governor Browning and the Philippines" is from Federal Judge Thomas Wiseman, speech delivered at West End United Methodist Church, Nashville, 1988.

"Gordon Browning and Alvin York" is from Larry Daughtrey, as told to Roy Herron, Dec. 1999.

"Gordon Browning and His Bride" is from Majors, *The End of Arcadia,* 148, 152, and 234.

"Governor Clement's Public Speaking" is from Lee Seifert Greene, *Lead Me On: Frank Goad Clement and Tennessee Politics* (Knoxville: Univ. of Tennessee Press, 1982), 29.

"Governor Clement's Oratory" is from Greene, *Lead Me On,* 378.

"Governor Clement and Roads" is from Roy Herron, personal recollection from an unknown source.

"Tennessee Colonels" is from Greene, *Lead Me On,* 121.

"Governor Clement and Mountain City" is from Roy Herron, personal recollection from an unknown source, about 1984.

"Buford Ellington and Drue Smith" is from Tom Humphrey, as told to Roy Herron, Jan. 1999.

"Governor Alexander, President Reagan, and Speaker McWherter's Fencing" is from Billy Stair, as told to Roy Herron, Dec. 13, 1997.

"McWherter's Smooth as Butter" is from Clay Wilson, as told to Roy Herron, July 1985.

"Governor McWherter's Suggestions" is from Cotton Ivy, personal recollection.

"Governor McWherter and the Freshman Legislator" is from Roy Herron, personal recollection, 1994.

"McWherter's Tough Game" is from Billy Stair, as told to Roy Herron, Dec. 13, 1997.

"Governor McWherter's Warmth in Winter" is from Josephine Binkley, as told to Roy Herron, Dec. 1992.

"McWherter's Sympathy" is from Cotton Ivy, personal recollection, Feb. 1994.

"Governor McWherter's Crowd" is from Roy Herron, personal recollection.

"The Difference between Being Governor and Chairman" is from Cotton Ivy, personal recollection.

"McWherter Driving Again" is from Cotton Ivy, personal recollection.

6. JUDICIAL BRANCH

"Justice Joe Henry" is from Justice William H. D. Fones, "In Honor of Joseph W. Henry: The Best of Joe," *Tennessee Law Review* (Summer 1980): 681–87, and Fred Travis, "Justice Joe Henry's Sense of Humor," *Chattanooga Times,* 14 June 1980, D-3.

"The Classic Cat II" is from *Metropolitan Government of Nashville v. Martin,* 584 S.W. 2d 643 (1979).

"Justice Henry's Circus Cannonballer" is from *Tennessee Law Review,* 6 Sept. 1976, 686.

"Justice John Wilkes" is from "A Tribute to the Memory of Honorable John S. Wilkes," 199 Tenn. 745–55, and Kirk Loggins, "Henry-Court's Social Conscience," *Nashville Tennessean,* 10 June 1980, 1.

"The Suicidal Pony" is from *Lyons v. Stills,* 37 S.W. 280, 97 Tenn. 514 (1896).

"The Mare and the Train" is from *Southern Railway Company v. Phillips,* 42 S.W. 925, 100 Tenn. 130 (1897).

"Thoroughly Trained Coon Dogs" is from *Fink et al. v. Evans,* 32 S.W. 307, 95 Tenn. 13 (1895).

"Knoxville's Disorderly, Incarcerated Mule" is from *Mincey v. Bradburn,* 56 S.W. 273, 103 Tenn. 407 (1899).

"Judge Andrew Jackson" is from Justice Riley Anderson, "We Share a Common Bond," *Tennessee Bar Journal* (Mar./Apr. 1997): 10–16.

"Evans Smith's Suits" is from a Henry countian who prefers to remain unnamed.

"Evans Smith's Shoats" is from a Henry countian who prefers to remain unnamed.

"Aaron Brown and 'Cutworm' Pierce" is from a Henry countian who prefers to remain unnamed.

"I Can't Hear" is from Tommy Thomas, as told to Roy Herron, 1998.

"East Tennessee Justice" is from Cotton Ivy, personal recollection.

"Justice, Tires, We Do It All" is from Judge David Hayes, Court of Criminal Appeals, as told to Roy Herron, 1995.

"Magazine Law" is from Judge David Hayes, Court of Criminal Appeals, as told to Roy Herron, 1995.

"Not Settling for Apples," is from *National Law Journal,* 9 Jan. 1989, 35.

"Judge Weinman for the Defense" is from Bill Haltom, as told to Roy Herron, 1987.

"Who Gets the Mule?" is from Bill Haltom, *Memphis Bar Association Magazine* (1993): 7.

7. NATIONAL GOVERNMENT

"Senator Baker's Landing" is from Larry Daughtrey, as told to Roy Herron, Dec. 1999.

"Senator McKellar and the Founding of Oak Ridge" is from Frist and Annis, *Tennessee Senators, 29.*

"National Candidates" is from Greene, *Lead Me On, 238.*

"Senator Kefauver and 'How's Your Dad?'" is from Frist and Annis, *Tennessee Senators, 85.*

"Al Gore Sr. and the Honorable Gentlemen" is from Hardy Mays, as told to Roy Herron, Feb. 1998.

"Senator Albert Gore Sr. and the Boys" is from Jerry Futrell and Gordon Oldham, as told to Roy Herron, Oct. 1989.

"Albert Gore's Strawberries" is from "Al Bissell as We Remembered Him at the League," *Tennessee Town & City,* 20 June 1994, 12.

"Senator Howard Baker Jr. and Mayor Al Bissell" is from "Al Bissell as We Remembered Him at the League," *Tennessee Town & City,* 20 June 1994, 12.

"Congressman Quillen's Poker-Playing Sheriff" is from Jimmy Quillen, as told to Cotton Ivy, 1987.

"Congressman Jones, Senator Sasser, and Speaker O'Neill" is from Cotton Ivy, personal recollection from the 1980s.

"Like Mister Ed" is from Joe Hill, as told to Roy Herron, 1995.

"Hadn't Planned on Going That High" is from Joe Hill, speech delivered in Haywood County, Sept. 1999.

"The John Tanner Statue" is from Joe Hill, as told to Roy Herron, 1995.

"Southern Speakers" is from *Nashville Tennessean,* 26 June 1997, 8A.

"Vice President Gore's Waiter" is from a speech by Al Gore Jr. given in May 1993.

"Gore on Republicans and Democrats" is from a speech by Al Gore Jr. given in May 1993.

"Tipper Gore's Titles" is from a speech by Tipper Gore given to supporters in Nashville, Mar. 1996.

8. ONE-LINERS

"Politics" is from Tommy Alexander, speech at Dresden, May 1998.

"Why Washington Told the Truth" is from John Bragg, as told to Roy Herron, 1995.

"Future Congressman" is from Alexander, *Steps Along the Way,* 101.

"Regardless" is from Greene, *Lead Me On,* 135.

"Choosing Words" is from Alexander, *Steps Along the Way,* 86.

"Baker's Gift" is from Alexander, *Steps Along the Way,* 32.

"Baker's Advice" is from Lamar Alexander, *Selections from Lamar Alexander's Little Plaid Book* (Nashville: Rutledge Hill, 1998), 33.

"Lots of Governors But Only One Dolly" is from Alexander, selections from Lamar Alexander's *Little Plaid Book,* 31.

"McWherter's Not Opposing" is from *Tennessee Journal,* 4 Apr. 1994, 4.

"Touched" is from *Tennessee Journal,* 24 Oct. 1994, 4.

"Sasser on Quayle" is from a speech by Senator James Sasser, Oct. 1992.

"Gore and Quayle" is from *Tennessee Journal,* 29 July 1992, 4.

"Gore's Code Name" is from *Tennessee Journal,* 4 Apr. 1994, 4.

"The Source of Wisdom" is from a speech by Al Gore Jr. given in Mar. 1989.

"A Slow-Growing Tree" is from a speech by Al Gore Jr. given in Mar. 1989.

"On Democratic Unity—or the Lack Thereof" is from a speech by Al Gore Jr. given in Mar. 1989.

"Love in the House" is from Roy Herron, personal recollection.

"24,000 Boos" is from Alexander, *Steps Along the Way,* 87.

"They're Here" is from Joe Hill, as told to Roy Herron, 1994.

"On the Electorate" is from Charles Curtiss, as told to Roy Herron, Oct. 1999.

"Cinderella" is from *Nashville Tennessean,* 26 June 1997, 8A.

"Hank vs. Fate, Fidelity vs. Fatback" is from Bruce Dobie, ed., *You Are So Nashville If . . . By the Readers of the* Nashville Scene (Nashville: Rutledge Hill Press, 1998), 12.

"Gridiron Politicians" is from speeches by Terry Keeter, Apr. 1988, and Apr. 1996.

9. DAVY CROCKETT

"Not a Boy, Nor a Goat" is from James Shackford, *David Crockett: The Man and the Legend* (Lincoln: Univ. of Nebraska Press, 1956), 20–21.

"Reports of Crockett's Death" is from David Crockett, *A Narrative of The Life of David Crockett of the State of Tennessee* (1834; reprint, Knoxville: Univ. of Tennessee Press, 1973) 127–32, quotation on 132.

"The Father" is from Crockett, *Narrative,* 126–27, and James Burke, *David Crockett: The Man Behind the Myth* (Austin, Tex.: Eakin Press, 1984), 103.

"Running for Colonel" is from Shackford, *David Crockett,* 39–40.

"The Legislative Candidate" is from Burke, *David Crockett,* 108.

"The Campaigner" is from Shackford, *David Crockett,* 167, and Crockett, *Narrative,* 166–69.

"The Bear Hunter" is from Crockett, *Narrative,* 194, 175–76, 190–91.

"The Defeated Candidate's Explanation" is from Shackford, *David Crockett,* 74.

"Congressional Candidate" is from Herbert Harper, ed., *Houston and Crockett: Heroes of Tennessee and Texas: An Anthology* (Nashville: Tennessee Historical Commission, 1986), 159, and Shackford, *David Crockett,* 74.

"Congressman Crockett's First Session" is from Harper, *Houston and Crockett,* 161.

"Name Calling" is from Harper, *Houston and Crockett,* 172.

"Yankee Teasing and Southern Wit" is from Harper, *Houston and Crockett,* 187.

"Another Campaign" is from Shackford, *David Crockett,* 83.

"The Break with President Jackson" is from Shackford, *David Crockett,* 131 and 140.

"The Last Campaign" is from Shackford, *David Crockett,* 203–4.

"The Departure" is from Shackford, *David Crockett,* xi and 212.

10. PICKIN COTTON

These stories were recorded during performances by Cotton Ivy. Many were recorded in about 1986 during one performance that became an audiotape called "Politics and Cotton."

Bibliography

NEWSPAPER AND MAGAZINE ARTICLES

Anderson, Riley. "We Share a Common Bond." *Tennessee Bar Journal* (Mar./ Apr. 1997).

"Al Bissell as We Remembered Him at the League." *Tennessee Town & City,* 20 June 1994.

Catalano, Gen. Michael W. "*Kidd v. McCanless:* The Genesis of Reappointment Litigation in Tennessee." *Tennessee Historical Quarterly* 44 (Spring 1985).

Cheek, Duran. "Casket Legislation Comes Alive in House Debate." *Nashville Tennessean,* 7 Mar. 1996.

"Cooper's 4th District Bid Gives Business Lobbies Headache." *Nashville Tennessean,* 22 June 1998.

"Ed Crump, 'Master of the Put-down' and How He Did It to Gov. Browning." *Tennessee Town and City,* 11 May 1987.

Fones, Justice William H. D. "In Honor of Joseph W. Henry: The Best of Joe." *Tennessee Law Review* (Summer 1980).

Halrom, Bill. *Memphis Bar Association Magazine* (1993).

Humphrey, Tom. "Notebook." *Knoxville News-Sentinel,* 30 Apr. 1995.

"Justice Henry's Circus Cannonballer." *Tennessee Law Review,* 6 Sept. 1976.

Loggins, Kirk. "Henry-Court's Social Conscience." *Nashville Tennessean,* 10 June 1980.

"Not Settling for Apples," *National Law Journal,* 9 Jan. 1989.

Tennessee Journal, 4 Apr. 1994.

Travis, Fred. "Justice Joe Henry's Sense of Humor." *Chattanooga Times,* 14 June 1980.

UT Torchbearer (University of Tennessee alumni magazine) (Spring 1987).

COURT OPINIONS

Fink et al. v. Evans, 32 S.W. 307, 95 Tenn. 13 (1895).

Lyons v. Stills, 37 S.W. 280, 97 Tenn. 514 (1896).

Mincey v. Bradburn, 56 S.W. 273, 103 Tenn. 407 (1899).

Southern Railway Company v. Phillips, 42 S.W. 925, 100 Tenn. 130 (1897).

BOOKS

Alexander, Lamar. *Steps Along the Way.* Nashville, Tenn.: Thomas Nelson, 1986.

Bergeron, Paul H., Stephen V. Ash, and Jeanette Keith. *Tennesseans and Their History.* Knoxville: Univ. of Tennessee Press, 1999.

Bowles, Billy, and Remer Tyson. *They Love a Man in the Country.* Memphis, Tenn.: Peachtree, 1989.

Boyce, Everett Robert, ed. *The Unwanted Boy: The Autobiography of Governor Ben W. Hooper.* Knoxville: Univ. of Tennessee Press, 1963.

Brown, Wilmore, ed. *The Legal Architect.* Charlottesville, Va.: Michie, 1959.

Burke, James. *David Crockett: The Man Behind the Myth.* Austin, Tex.: Eakin Press, 1984.

Caro, Robert A. *The Path to Power.* New York: Knopf, 1982.

Corlew, Robert E. *Tennessee: A Short History,* 2d ed. Knoxville: Univ. of Tennessee Press, 1981.

Crockett, David. *A Narrative of the Life of David Crockett of the State of Tennessee.* 1834. Reprint, Knoxville: Univ. of Tennessee Press, 1973.

Dobie, Bruce, ed. *You Are So Nashville If . . . By the Readers of the* Nashville Scene. Nashville: Rutledge Hill Press, 1998.

Ewing, James. *A Treasury of Tennessee Tales.* Nashville, Tenn.: Rutledge Hill Press, 1985.

Frist, William H., and J. Lee Annis Jr. *Tennessee Senators.* New York: Madison Books, 1999.

Gorman, Joseph Bruce. *Kefauver: A Political Biography.* New York: Oxford Univ. Press, 1971.

Greene, Lee Seifert. *Lead Me On: Frank Goad Clement and Tennessee Politics.* Knoxville: Univ. of Tennessee Press, 1982.

Harper, Herbert, ed. *Houston and Crockett: Heroes of Tennessee and Texas: An Anthology.* Nashville: Tennessee Historical Commission, 1986.

Majors, William. *The End of Arcadia.* Memphis: Memphis State Univ. Press, 1982.

May, John G., Jr., *The Lighter Side of the Law.* Charlottesville, Va.: Michie, 1956.

McClay, John B., and Wendy L. Matthews, eds. *Corpus Juris Humorous.* New York: Macmillan/McGraw-Hill, 1991.

McMurty, J. C. *Humor in Tennessee Justice.* Tompkinsville, Ky.: Monroe County Press, 1979.

Neider, Charles, ed. *The Comic Mark Twain.* New York: Doubleday, 1977.

Shackford, James. *David Crockett: The Man and the Legend.* Lincoln: Univ. of Nebraska Press, 1956.

Vile, John R., and Mark Byrnes, eds. *Tennessee Government and Politics: Democracy in the Volunteer State.* Nashville, Tenn.: Vanderbilt Univ. Press, 1998.

West, Carroll Van, et al., eds. *The Tennessee Encyclopedia of History and Culture.* Nashville: Tennessee Historical Society, 1998.

Index

Tennessee Political Humor was designed and typeset on a Macintosh computer system using PageMaker software. The text is set in Garamond 3 and the chapter openings are set in Potrzebie. This book was designed and typeset by Sheila Hart and manufactured by Thomson-Shore, Inc. The paper used in this book is designed for an effective life of at least three hundred years.

A Confession and an Invitation

We know many funny stories from Tennessee politics are not in this slim volume. If you did not find your favorite story here, call us or send it so we can include your story in the next book. If the editors let us include it (just as citizens blame politicians, writers blame editors), we will give you a copy as thanks for your contribution.

Also, let us know if you want to be notified when the second volume appears or if you would like books (signed or unsigned, as you prefer) for those hard-to-buy-for folks on your gift list.

We can be reached at:

Roy Herron and Cotton Ivy
P. O. Box 5
Dresden, TN 38225
731-364-5415
rherron@crunet.com